THROUGH THE GATE

OF

MY BOOK HOUSE

EDITED BY

OLIVE BEAUPRÉ MILLER

PUBLISHERS

THE BOOK HOUSE for CHILDREN

CHICAGO

PRINTED IN U.S.A.

CONTENTS

Translated by William Makepeace Thackery

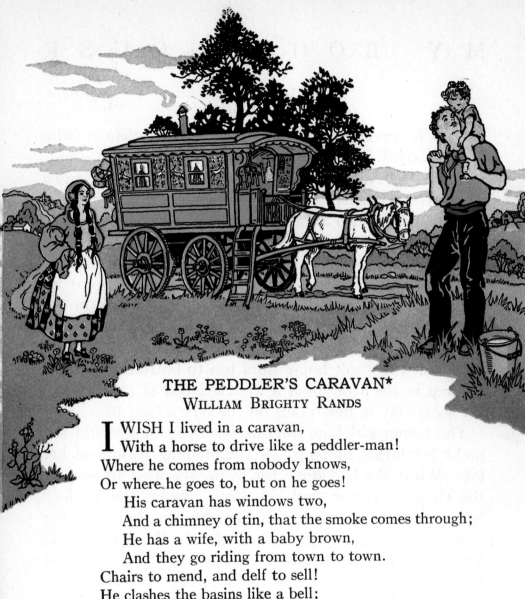

THE PEDDLER'S CARAVAN*
WILLIAM BRIGHTY RANDS

I WISH I lived in a caravan,
With a horse to drive like a peddler-man!
Where he comes from nobody knows,
Or where he goes to, but on he goes!
   His caravan has windows two,
   And a chimney of tin, that the smoke comes through;
   He has a wife, with a baby brown,
   And they go riding from town to town.
Chairs to mend, and delf to sell!
He clashes the basins like a bell;
Tea trays, baskets ranged in order,
Plates, with alphabets 'round the border!
   With the peddler-man I should like to roam,
   And write a book when I come home;
   All the people would read my book
   Just like the travels of Captain Cook!

*Used by the courteous permission of John Lane Company.

Cinderella*

Adapted from Perrault

ONCE upon a time there was a gentleman who married for his second wife, the proudest, vainest, and most selfish woman that ever was seen. She had two daughters, who were exactly like her in all things. The gentleman had also a daughter, but she was a young girl of the rarest sweetness and goodness. The mother could not bear the goodness of this young girl because it made the pride and ill-temper of her own daughters appear all the more ugly, so she gave her the hardest work in the house to do, in order that none of their visitors might notice her. She had to scour the dishes, scrub the floors, and clean the whole house from top to bottom. She had to sleep in the attic upon a wretched bed of straw, while her sisters lay in fine rooms on the very softest beds.

The young girl bore all this patiently, nor would she make her father unhappy by complaining to him of her lot. When she had done her work, she used to go into the chimney corner and sit down among the cinders; hence, though her name was Ella, she was called by her sisters, Cinderella. Cinderella had only the poorest rags for clothes, but the sweetness and goodness that shone in her face, made her a hundred-times more beautiful than her sisters, however richly they might be dressed.

It once happened that the King's son gave a very grand ball, to which all the great people of the kingdom were

---

*"Cinderella," comes from a French book, *Tales of My Mother Goose*, published by Charles Perrault, in 1699. These stories, centuries old, were told Perrault by an old nurse and translated into English, in 1729.

invited. Our young misses were highly delighted to receive an invitation. At once they began to busy themselves in choosing the gowns, petticoats, and headdresses which they would wear. Poor little Cinderella was not invited; yet, as she worked to get her sisters ready to go, they talked the whole day long of nothing but what they would do at the ball.

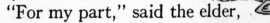

"For my part," said the elder, "I shall wear my blue velvet suit with French trimmings."

"And I," said the younger, "shall wear my old skirt, but then to make up for that, I shall put on my gold-flowered mantle and my splendid diamond stomacher."

At last the happy day came. Though Cinderella was sad to think she must stay at home, she offered very sweetly to dress her sisters' hair; but, even as she worked, they said unkind things to her.

"Cinderella, don't you wish you could go to the ball? How people would laugh to see a cinder-girl at a ball!"

Cinderella made no answer. She went on arranging their hair. So at last she had them looking as well as two young misses could, whose faces expressed nothing but pride and ill-temper. They paraded up and down

before the long mirrors in their rooms, and then they got into the family coach and drove away to court.

Cinderella looked after them until they were far out of sight; then she crept into her corner by the chimney and fell softly a-crying. But Cinderella, like all good girls, was watched over by a fairy godmother; and, as she sat there in tears, her good fairy appeared before her.

"My dear, dear child," said the queer little old lady, "why are you crying?"

"I wish—I wish—I wish —I could—," Cinderella could not finish for sobbing.

"You wish," said the Fairy, "that you could go to the ball. Is not that so?"

"Yes! Oh, yes!" answered Cinderella, sighing.

"Well," said the Fairy, "be but a good girl, and I will see that you go." Then she commanded the dear child to run into the garden and bring her a pumpkin. Cinderella went obediently and gathered the finest she could find, though she hadn't the smallest idea how a pumpkin could help her get to the ball. Her fairy godmother scooped out all the inside, leaving nothing but the rind; then she struck it with her wand and behold! the pumpkin became a splendid, gilded coach!

Next, the fairy godmother went to look into the mouse-traps where she found six mice. She ordered Cinderella to lift the door of each trap and, as the mouse ran out, she gave it a tap with her wand. At once the mouse was changed into a horse, till before them stood six fine horses of a beautiful, mouse-colored gray. Then she had Cinder-

MARGUERITE DAVIS

15

ella bring her the rattrap. In that was a very large rat with splendid whiskers and she turned him into a coachman. Last of all, she said:

"Go into the garden, Cinderella, and bring me the six lizards you will find behind the watering-pot."

No sooner had Cinderella done as she was commanded, than the lizards became six footmen in gold-embroidered coats. They skipped up at once behind the coach and sat there as grandly as though they had done nothing all their lives but serve in such a position.

The fairy then said to Cinderella, "Now you see a carriage fit to take you to the ball."

"Oh, yes, thank you!" cried Cinderella.

And the godmother touched her with her wand; and, at that same moment, her clothes were turned into cloth of gold and silver, all decked with jewels. Then the fairy gave her a pair of the prettiest glass slippers in the world, and said, as she stepped joyously into the carriage:

"This one command only you must obey. Do not on any account stay at the ball after midnight. If you do, your coach will become a pumpkin again, your horses, mice; your coachman, a rat; your footmen, lizards; and your clothes, the same rags you wore before."

Cinderella promised to obey and then she drove away. The King's son, being told that a great princess whom nobody knew was come to the ball, ran out to receive her. He gave her his hand as she alighted from the coach, and led her into the hall where the company was gathered. At once when she appeared, there fell over all a deep silence; every one left off dancing and the violins ceased to play. On all sides ladies and gentlemen whispered, "How beautiful she is!"

The King's son conducted her to the seat of honor, and afterwards led her out to dance. She danced so gracefully that all admired her. She was kind and courteous, too, even to her ill-tempered stepsisters, who did not for a moment recognize in this lovely princess their little cinder-girl. At last a splendid feast was served; but, in the midst of it all, Cinderella heard the clock strike the quarter before twelve. She rose and said farewell. Then she hastened away.

When she got back home, she found her godmother waiting. Gratefully she thanked the little old lady for what she had done. But as she was telling her all that had happened, her two sisters knocked at the door. Then the fairy changed Cinderella's brocaded gown to rags again and disappeared in a twinkling. In her poor old clothes, Cinderella opened the door.

"If you had been at the ball," said one of her sisters, "you would have seen the finest, most beautiful Princess that ever your eyes looked on. She was very kind to us, too, and showed us much attention. But a little cinder-girl like you could never even dream of such beauty!"

Cinderella asked if they knew the name of the Princess.

"No," the stepsisters answered, "no one knows her name but the King's son would give all the world to know!"

The next night the Prince asked everyone again to
a ball that he might once more see the beautiful
Princess. Cinderella's two sisters went and, when they
were gone and the house was still, her godmother came
as before and made Cinderella ready. The dress she
wore on the second night was even more lovely than the
one she had had at first. The King's son welcomed her
with beaming eyes and was always by her side. They
danced with the same grace and beauty to the same lovely
music. And they feasted as before. But, when the clock
struck a quarter to twelve, Cinderella remembered her
godmother's words and went obediently home.

The third night the King's son gave still another ball;
once again the two sisters went and after them, Cinderella.

THROUGH THE GATE

Not a thing was less fine and splendid than on the two nights preceding. Indeed, the music was so beautiful, the room was so bright, and everything was so full of joy, that Cinderella never once thought how time was flying.

Suddenly, the clock of the palace began to strike. One! Two! Three! Four! When she heard, Cinderella fled. Nimbly as a deer she ran. Five! Six! Seven! Eight! She was on the broad steps outside the palace. Nine! Ten! One little glass slipper fell from her foot, but she dared not stop to pick it up. Eleven! Twelve! Her clothes all turned to rags! Her coach disappeared! Mice, lizards, and rat scampered off in the darkness. As fast as she could, Cinderella ran home. All she had left of her finery was one little glass slipper, the mate to the one she had lost.

In great dismay, the Prince ran out from the palace after her. Not a sign of her was anywhere to be seen. The guards at the gate said no splendid Princess had passed them. They had seen nobody but a poorly-dressed country girl, who ran as if for her life.

The Prince was very sorrowful and he had a search made everywhere. But all he could find of the beautiful Princess was the one little glass slipper she had dropped. For days and days he searched; then at last he had his servitors march up and down through the length and breadth of his kingdom, giving notice with sound of trumpet that every lady in the land should try on the little glass slipper. So small it

BILLIE·PARKS

was, he knew that none but the rightful princess could wear it. Hence he gave orders that whoever could get her foot into it, should straightway become his bride.

They began by trying the slipper on the princesses, then on the duchesses, and then on the other ladies of the court; not one of them did it fit. At last it was brought to Cinderella's two proud sisters, who each did all she could to squeeze in her foot; they pinched up their heels and drew in their toes, but in vain. Cinderella, meantime, stood by and watched what was going on. She knew her slipper; and, when her sisters had failed, she said to them modestly: "Let me see if it will not fit me."

The sisters burst out laughing. "Could a cinder-girl wear such a slipper?" they cried. But the mes-

senger who was sent out on the search, finding Cinderella very beautiful, said it was but fair she should try it. So Cinderella sat down, and the gentleman put the slipper to her foot. Behold! it went on easily and fitted her like wax. The two sisters were dumb with amazement, but their amazement was greater still when Cinderella pulled out of her pocket the mate to that beautiful slipper. Thereupon, in came her good fairy, who touched the girl's clothes with her wand, and lo! they became more magnificent than any she had worn before.

And now her two sisters found her to be that beautiful lady who had been so kind to them at the ball. They threw themselves at her feet to beg pardon for all their ill-treatment of her. Cinderella lifted them up, kissed them, and said she forgave them with all her heart.

She was conducted to the young prince, dressed as she was. He thought her more charming than ever. A few days later he led her, as his bride, to live with him at the palace. Cinderella, who was as good as she was beautiful, gave her two sisters a home at court. Henceforth, they were kinder women.

THE PUMPKIN

John Greenleaf Whittier

WE'VE laughed round the corn-
heap with hearts all in tune
Our chair a broad pumpkin—our lantern the moon.
Telling tales of the fairy who travelled like steam
In a pumpkin shell coach with two rats for her team.

Doll i' the Grass

A Norse Folk Tale

ONCE upon a time there was a King who had twelve sons. When they were grown up, he told them that they must go out into the world and find themselves wives. These wives, he commanded, must be able to spin, weave, and make a shirt in a day, else he would not have them for daughters-in-law. So the sons all set out into the world to look for brides.

When they had traveled a bit on the way, they said that they would not take Ashiepattle, their youngest brother, with them, for he was good for nothing. So they left the poor youth behind. Ashiepattle got off his horse, sat down in the grass and began to weep.

When he had sat there a while, lo! one of the tussocks among the grass began to stir and move, and out of it came a small white thing. Ashiepattle's mouth fell open with astonishment. But as the white thing came nearer, he saw it was a charming little lassie, such a tiny bit of a thing, so very, very tiny.

She came up to him and asked him if he would go below with her and pay a visit to the Doll i' the Grass. Yes, he  would; and so he did. When he came down below, the Doll i' the Grass was sitting in a chair, dressed very finely and looking very beautiful. She asked Ashiepattle whither he was going and what was his errand.

He told her that he was one of twelve brothers, and that the King had given them each a horse and a suit of armor, bidding them go out into the world and find themselves wives. "But," said he, "each wife must be able to spin, weave, and make a shirt in a day. If you can do that and will marry me, I will not go a step farther."

So the Doll i' the Grass set to work at once to get the shirt spun, woven, and made, but when it was done, it was so tiny, no bigger than—so!

Ashiepattle took it and returned home. When he brought it out to show his father, he felt very shy because it was so small. But for all it was so tiny, it was perfectly made, so the King said he would be glad to have the lady who had made it become his daughter-in-law. You can imagine how happy and joyful Ashiepattle was then.

The road did not seem long to him as he set out to fetch his little bride. When he came to the Doll i' the Grass, he wanted to take her up before him on his horse; but no, that she wouldn't; she said she would sit and drive in a silver spoon, and she had two small white horses which would draw her.

So they set out, he on his horse and she in the silver spoon, and the horses which drew her were two small white mice. Ashiepattle always kept to one side of the road, so that he would not ride over her; she was so tiny.

When they had traveled a bit on the way, they came to a large pond; there Ashiepattle's horse shied and up-set the spoon, so that the Doll i' the Grass tumbled into the water. Ashiepattle was most sorrowful, for he did not know how he could get her out again; but after a while up came a merman with her. And now she had

become just as big as any other grown person and far lovelier than before. So Ashiepattle placed her before him on his horse and rode home.

When he got there all his brothers had also returned, each with a bride; but, though they had thought themselves so much better than Ashiepattle and left him behind, they had all chosen brides who were ugly, ill-favored, and bad-tempered. On their heads these young misses had hats which were painted with tar and soot, and this had run down their faces, making them still uglier to behold. The King was so overjoyed with Ashiepattle and his bride that he sent the others about their business, and said Ashiepattle should be king after him. So Ashiepattle and Doll i' the Grass held the wedding feast and they lived long and happily together.

The Twelve Dancing Princesses
A German Folk Tale

THERE was once a King who had twelve beautiful daughters and they slept in twelve beds, all in one room. When they went to bed, the doors were shut and locked, but every morning their shoes were found to be quite worn through as if they had been danced in all night long; yet nobody could ever find out where the maidens had been. At last the King declared that, if any young man could discover the secret, he should have the princess he liked best for his bride; but whoever tried and did not succeed after three nights, should be beaten and driven out of the kingdom.

A King's son soon came. He was well-entertained; and, in the evening, was taken to the chamber next to the one where the princesses lay in their twelve beds. There he was to sit and watch. In order that nothing might pass without his hearing it, the door of his chamber was left open. But the King's son soon fell asleep. When he awoke in the morning, he found that the princesses had all been dancing, for the soles of their shoes were full of holes—yet he knew no more than before where they had been. The same thing happened the second night and the third. Each time the Prince fell asleep and learned nothing, so the King ordered him to be beaten and driven out of the kingdom. After him came several others, but they all went to sleep just as he had done and did not learn the secret; so they, too, were driven away in disgrace. So severe were these punishments that soon no more kings' sons presented themselves for the task.

Then it happened that a plain man who had always worked for his living, came to the country where this King reigned. As he was traveling through a wood, the youth met an old woman who asked him where he was going. "I should like very much to go to the castle and find out where it is that the princesses dance," said the youth, "then I might win one of them for my bride."

"Well," said the dame, "this is the secret of finding out—keep awake! Keep awake and watch!"

Then she gave him a cloak and she said, "If you are listening carefully, you will hear the noise of their going. Then put on this coat; it will make you invisible and you will be able to go straight through the wall and follow them. Only mind you, do not let sleep overcome you or you will be lost." The youth listened attentively to this good counsel, then he went to the King and said he was willing to undertake the task.

The King received him well and, when the evening came, he was led to the outer chamber. But the princesses, hearing him enter the room, laughed heartily. "This fellow will do as the rest have done," said the eldest. "In a moment he will be snoring!" But the youth did nothing of the kind. He waited, every moment on guard. It was about midnight when the twelve princesses rose, opened their drawers and boxes, took out all their fine clothes, dressed themselves at the glass, and skipped about, eager to begin dancing. The youth listened till he heard the noise of their preparations cease, as though they were ready to go, then he quickly put on the cloak which the old woman had given him, and hurried into their chamber. Just as he arrived in the room, the eldest went up to her own bed and clapped her hands; at that the bed sank into the floor and a trap door flew open. Then the youth saw the twelve princesses go down through the trap door one after another, the eldest leading the way. He followed them so closely that, in the middle of the stairs along which they were passing, he trod on the gown of the youngest princess.

"All is not right, some one touched my gown!" she cried. "You silly creature," said the eldest, "it is nothing but a nail in the wall." So down they all went and, at the bottom,

they found themselves in a most delightful grove of trees; the leaves were all of silver that glittered and sparkled beautifully. The youth wished to take away some token of the place to show the King, so he broke off a little branch and there came a loud noise from the tree. Then the youngest princess said again, "I am sure all is not right—did not you hear that noise? That never happened before." But the eldest said, "It is only our princes shouting for joy at our approach." Soon they came to another grove of trees where all the leaves were of gold, and afterward, to a third with leaves of glittering diamonds. The youth broke a branch from each; and every time he did so, there came a loud snapping, which made the youngest princess cry out that something was the matter. But in spite of her words, they all kept on till they came to a lake where twelve little boats were floating; and, in the boats were twelve handsome princes, who seemed to be awaiting the princesses.

One of the princesses stepped into each boat and the invisible young man got into the boat with the youngest. As they were crossing the lake the prince who was rowing the youngest said, "I do not know why it is, but the boat seems very heavy tonight."

On the other side of the lake stood a brightly lighted castle, from which came the sound of merry music. There they all landed and went into the castle. Each prince danced with his princess; and the youth, who was all the time invisible, followed the youngest princess about, for he found her very lovely indeed. They danced on thus till four o'clock in the morning; then all their shoes were worn out, so they were obliged to leave off. The princes rowed them back again over the lake, and once more the youth took his place in the boat, close beside the youngest princess. On the opposite shore the princes took leave of the maidens, the princesses promising to come again the next night.

When they came to the stairs, the youth ran on ahead and jumped into bed; so, when the twelve sisters came up, he was already asleep and snoring.

"You see he has been sleeping all this time just as the others did and has seen nothing," they said.

Then they undressed themselves, put away their fine clothes, pulled off their shoes, and went to bed. In the morning the youth said nothing about what had happened, but determined to see more of this strange adventure. Again the second and third nights, he followed the maidens. Everything happened just as before; the princesses danced each time till their shoes were all worn to shreds and then returned home.

As soon as the time came when he must either declare the secret or be beaten out of the kingdom, he was taken before the King. With him he carried the three branches from the trees. When the King asked him, "Where do my twelve daughters dance at night?" he answered, "With twelve princes in a castle underground." Then he told the King all that had happened, and showed him the branches of silver, gold, and diamonds.

The King at once called for the princesses and when they found that their secret had been discovered, they told their father all about it. Then the King said, "My young man, it is good to be wide awake and watchful and know what is going on in this world!" And he asked the youth which of the maidens he would choose for his bride. The youth answered, "I will take the youngest."

So he did, and they lived happily ever after.

Snow-white and Rose-red
WILHELM AND JACOB GRIMM*

A POOR widow once lived in a little cottage that had a garden in front of it, and in this garden grew two beautiful rose trees. One of these trees bore white roses and the other red. Now the good woman had two children who were just like the rose trees. One was named Snow-white and the other Rose-red, and they were the sweetest, kindest, most industrious and cheerful little maids in all the world. Rose-red loved to run and skip over fields and meadows, picking nosegays of flowers, and chasing the beautiful butterflies, but Snow-white was quieter and more gentle than her sister. She remained at home with her mother, either helping her with her work or reading aloud to her when their work was done. The two children loved each other so dearly that they always went hand in hand whenever they were out together; and, if Snow-white said to her sister, "We will never leave each other," Rose-red always answered, "No, not while we live." Then the mother

*Wilhelm and Jacob Grimm, the first great collectors of folk tales, wandered through Germany about 1800, taking down from old grannies and country folk, tales told by the people for centuries, but never written down.

would add, "Whatever one has, let her always share with the other."

They often roamed together in the woods, gathering berries, and no beast ever even offered to hurt them. On the contrary, all the animals came up to them in the most trustful and affectionate manner. The little hare would nibble a cabbage leaf from their very hands; the deer grazed beside them; the stag leaped past them joyous and free; the birds never stirred from their branches at their approach, but sang to them in perfect security. No evil ever befell them. If night overtook them in the wood, they laid themselves down on the moss and slept until morning, and their mother was satisfied they were safe and was never anxious about them.

Once when they had passed the night in the woods and were awakened by the bright morning sun, they saw a beautiful child in a shining white dress sitting close by their resting-place. She rose when they opened their eyes and looked at them kindly, but she said not a word and vanished from their sight. When the children looked about them, they saw that they had slept on the edge of a precipice, over which they would certainly have fallen, had they gone two steps farther in the darkness. Their mother told them that the beautiful child must have been the angel who watches over good children.

35

Snow-white and Rose-red kept their mother's cottage so clean and neat that it was a pleasure even to look into it. In the summer, Rose-red looked after the house and placed by her mother's bed, every morning before she awoke, a nosegay in which was a rose from each of the rose trees. In the winter, Snow-white lit the fire and put the kettle on after scouring it so that it shone like gold. In the evening when the snowflakes fell, the mother said, "Snow-white, go and bolt the door." Then they drew round the fire and the good woman read aloud to the children from a large book while the girls listened and busied themselves at spinning. Beside them lay a lamb and behind perched a little white dove with its head tucked under its wing.

One evening as they all sat thus cozily together, a knock was heard at the door as if someone desired to enter.

"Quick, Rose-red, open the door," said the mother. "It must be some traveler in need of shelter."

Rose-red accordingly shot back the bolt expecting to see a poor man, but it was no such thing—it was a bear who thrust his great, black head in at the open door. Rose-red cried out and sprang back, the lamb bleated, the dove fluttered her wings, and Snow-white hid herself behind her mother's bed. But the bear began to speak and said, "Don't be afraid. I will do you no harm. I am half-frozen and only wish to warm myself by your fire."

"Poor bear," said the mother, "lie down by the fire, only take care you don't burn your fur."

Then she called Snow-white and Rose-red to come out of their hiding-places. "This bear," she said, "is a good kind creature and will do you no harm." So the children obeyed and, by degrees, the lamb and the dove drew near too, and they all forgot their fear.

"Children," said the bear, "knock a little of the snow off my coat." So they fetched the broom and swept the bear's coat quite clean. After which he stretched himself out before the fire and growled quite happily and comfortably. Before long the children and the bear and the lamb and the dove were all good friends, and Snow-white and Rose-red began to sport with their unexpected guest, tugging at his thick fur or putting their feet on his back and rolling him over and over. Then they took a thin hazel twig and tickled him with it, and, when he growled, they laughed. The bear submitted to everything with the best possible good nature, only when they went a little too far, he cried, "Children, children, leave me an inch of my life!"

When night came and all prepared to go to bed, the widow said to the bear: "You can stay here and lie on the hearth all night if you like. It will shelter you from the cold and snow."

The bear accepted the offer gratefully, but as soon as the day dawned, the two children let him out and he trotted over the snow back into the woods.

From this time on, the bear came every evening at the same hour, laid himself down by the fire, and let the chil-

dren play whatever
pranks they liked
with him. Soon they
grew so attached to
their strange playfellow
that the door was never bolted of an evening until he
had made his appearance. But when spring came and
everything outside was green and bright, the bear said
one morning to Snow-white, "I must leave you now
and I will not be able to return all summer."

"Where are you going, dear bear?" asked Snow-white.

"I must go to the woods," answered the bear, "to
protect my treasure from the bad dwarfs. In the winter
when the ground is frozen hard, they are obliged to stay
shut up underground and cannot work their way out.
But now that the sun has thawed the earth, they find
their way up to the surface and are ever on the watch for
what they can steal; and whatever touches their hands or
reaches their caves rarely, if ever, sees daylight again."

Snow-white was very sorrowful when she took leave of
the good-natured beast and unbolted the door that he

might depart. In passing out, his fur was caught on a
hook and a bit was torn out. Snow-white fancied that
she saw something shine like gold underneath it, but he
passed out so quickly that she did not feel sure what it was;
and, in a twinkling, he had disappeared among the trees.

A short time after this, the mother sent her children
out into the woods to gather sticks. They soon came
upon a large tree which lay felled on the ground, and
among its roots, half-hidden by the grass, they saw something jumping and hopping about, but what it was they
could not make out. When they drew nearer, they saw
it was a dwarf with an old, withered face and a snow-
white beard a yard long. The end of the beard was caught
tight in a cleft in the tree and the little fellow was springing
backward and forward like a dog at the end
of a rope, but he could not get free. He
glared at the children with his fiery red
eyes and screamed out, "What are
you standing there for? Can't
you come and help me?"

"What have you been
doing?" asked Rose-red.

"You silly goose," cried
the dwarf, "I wanted to split
the tree that I might get
shavings for our kitchen.
Those great thick logs such
as are needed to cook the

great mountains of provisions that are devoured by coarse, greedy folk like you, would quite burn up the little food we cook. I had successfully driven in the wedge and should soon have done what I wanted, when the wedge sprang unexpectedly out of the cleft, which closed again quickly over the end of my beautiful white beard. So here I am stuck fast and I cannot get away. Stupid simpletons, why do you stand there and laugh and do nothing?"

In spite of the little man's ill-temper, the girls did all in their power to set him free, but in vain—the beard was wedged in far too firmly. "I will run and fetch someone to help," said Rose-red. "Idiot!" screeched the dwarf. "Why go and fetch more dunderheads? Here are two too many already! Can't you think of anything better?"

"Don't be so impatient!" said Snow-white. "I will try to do something else." And taking out her scissors, she snipped the end off the dwarf's beard, thus setting him free at once. But for all that did he say thank you? No! Never a bit of it!

"Drat you, you ninnies, for cutting my beautiful beard," he cried as soon as he felt himself free. And seizing a bag full of gold which was hidden among the roots of the tree, he made off into the woods without even so much as a backward look at the children who had helped him.

Shortly after this Snow-white and Rose-red went out to fish in the brook. As they drew near the water, they saw something that looked like a great grasshopper jumping toward the stream as though just about to leap in.

They ran to see what it could be and recognized the very same old dwarf.

"Where are you going?" asked Rose-red. "Surely you can't mean to jump into the water."

"I'm not such a fool!" screamed the dwarf. "Don't you see that that horrid fish is pulling me in?"

The little man had been sitting on the bank fishing when, unfortunately, the wind entangled his beard in the line. As a large fish directly afterward took the bait, the disagreeable little fellow was not strong enough to pull the creature out, so the fish got the upper hand and was dragging the dwarf in after it. Though he caught at every stick and twig within reach, that did not help him much; he was forced to follow every move of the fish and was in continual danger of being drawn into the water. The girls came up just in time and did all they could to disentangle his beard from the line, but in vain. Nothing was left to do, but use the scissors again. So Snow-white cut off a very small piece of the beard. But when the dwarf saw what the girls were about, he cried in a rage, "Is this the way you ruin a fellow's face? Blockheads! I wish you had lost your way before ever you came this road. Was it not enough to shorten my beard before but you must be spoiling it altogether?"

Then he fetched a bag of pearls that lay among the brushes, hobbled away, and vanished behind a stone.

It happened soon after this that the mother sent her children to town to buy thread, needles, ribbons, and lace. Their road led over a heath where great rocks lay scattered about. As they trudged along, their attention was soon drawn to a huge bird that hovered about above them. It circled nearer and nearer the earth, till at last it dashed suddenly down among a mass of rocks. At once they heard a sharp, piercing cry and running to the spot, they saw, to their horror, that the eagle had pounced upon their old acquaintance, the dwarf, and was about to carry him off. The tender-hearted children did not for a moment hesitate. Taking firm hold of the little man, they struggled stoutly to free him from the eagle, and after much rough handling on both sides, the dwarf remained at last safe in the hands of his courageous little friends, while the great bird flew away. But for all that, did the little old man say thank you? No! Never a bit of it! When he had in a degree recovered from the shock, he cried in his thin cracked voice, "Couldn't you have handled me more gently? Look at my little coat. It's all torn to shreds, you useless, awkward hussies."

He then seized a sack of precious stones and vanished under the rocks. The girls were by this time quite accustomed to his thankless manner, so they went on their way and did their errands in town. On their way home, as they were again passing the heath, they once more came unexpectedly upon the ugly dwarf. He had emptied out his sack of precious gems and was counting them over, for he never thought anyone would be crossing the heath so late. The setting sun shone on the brilliant stones and they gleamed and glittered so beautifully that the children stood still to admire them. The face of the dwarf grew scarlet with rage as he saw them.

"Greenhorns! What are you standing there gaping at?" he cried, and was about to make off to his cave when a loud growl suddenly stopped him. Out of the woods came a great black bear. The dwarf in a fright once more tried to escape to his hiding-place, but the bear was right upon him. Then the little man cried out in terror, "Dear Mr. Bear, I beg you spare me. I'll give you all my treasure. Only look at all those beautiful gems. What pleasure would you get from gob- bling up such a little fellow as I? You wouldn't even get a taste of me! But look at those two wicked girls. There, lay hold of them! They would be tender morsels and are as fat as quails—pray take

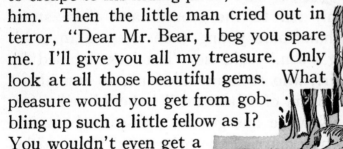

them, good Mr. Bear, and let me go!" The bear, however, was not to be moved by his words. He gave the evil, little creature one blow with his paw and that was the end of him once and for all.

In the meantime, the girls had run away toward home, but the bear called after them, "Snow-white, Rose-red, stop! Don't be afraid. I will go with you." Then they recognized his voice and stood still and, when the bear had come near them, the bearskin suddenly fell to the ground and there stood before them a handsome young man dressed in gold.

"I am a king's son," said he, "but was doomed by that wicked dwarf, who stole my treasure, to run about the woods in the form of a bear until I should be set free by his death. Now he has got his well-earned punishment." Snow-white married the prince and Rose-red his brother; and they divided between them the great treasure which the dwarf had collected in his cave. The good mother lived peacefully for many years with her children. But, when she left her cottage, she carried with her the two rose trees and they stood before her window and continued every year to bear the most beautiful red and white roses.

Elsa and the Ten Elves

A Swedish Fairy Tale

ONCE upon a time there was a pretty little girl named Elsa. She lived on a farm, but her father, who was very proud of her, sent her to school in the city. There she learned reading, writing, singing, dancing, and a number of other accomplishments, but she did not learn how to cook, sew, or care for a house. The truth of the matter was, that Elsa was lazy and did not like anything that she called work.

When she grew older, many young men wished her for a wife, but she chose her neighbour, Gunner, a handsome, industrious young farmer. So the two were married, and went to live on Gunner's farm.

At first they were very happy; but, as the days passed and Elsa did not direct the servants in their work or see that the house was kept in order, everything went wrong. The provisions in the storerooms were tumbled about, food was found missing, and the house was dirty. Poor Gunner was miserable, but he loved Elsa too much to say a word to her about it.

The day before Christmas came; the sun had been up and people bustling about the house for hours. Still Elsa lay fast asleep in her bed. At last a servant came.

"O mistress," she said, "the master and his men are ready to set off for the woods. What shall we pack in their lunch bags?"

"Don't talk to me," said Elsa sleepily.

Soon another servant came in. "The bread dough has risen," she cried. "If you come and knead it, the bread will be good." "Go away!" answered Elsa.

And so it went; servant after servant came running into the room asking for orders, but Elsa would only answer, "Go away!" and she would not get up.

At last Gunner could stand it no longer. There was the poor fellow with his men delayed in their start for the woods because no one knew what to pack for their luncheon. So off he went to Elsa's room.

"Dear Elsa," he said gently, "my mother used to prepare things the night before, so that the servants might begin work early in the morning. She did not lie in bed when the sun was up. My men and I are off now with I know not what in our lunch bags. Surely you are ready by this time to rise. Remember, there are a few yards of cloth on the loom waiting to be woven." Then Gunner went away.

THROUGH THE GATE

As soon as he was gone, Elsa got up grumbling. After she had dressed herself, she slowly ate her breakfast, and then went, loitering, off to the little house where the loom was kept. But when she got there, she slammed the door and threw herself down on a couch. "No!" she cried, half sobbing, "I won't do this weaving! Who would have thought that Gunner would make me work like a servant? Oh, me! Oh, me! Is there no one to help me?"

"I can help you," said a deep voice. Then Elsa, raising her head, saw an old man in a black cloak and a broad-brimmed hat, standing close by her side. "I am Old Man Hoberg," he said, "and have served your family for many years. You, my child, are unhappy because you are idle. To be idle makes any one miserable. I will give you ten obedient servants who shall do all your tasks for you."

At that he shook his long, black cloak, and out of its

47

folds tumbled ten queer little men. For a moment they capered and pranced about. Then they swiftly put the room in order and finished weaving the cloth on the loom. When their work was done, they ran up and stood in a row before Elsa, as though awaiting her orders.

"Dear child, reach out your hands," said the old man.

Trembling and uncertain, Elsa held out the tips of her fingers. Then he cried:

"Hop-o'-My-Thumb,
    Lick-the-Pot,
        Long-Pole,
            Heart-in-Hand,
                Little-Peter-Funny-Man,
                    Away all of you to your places!"

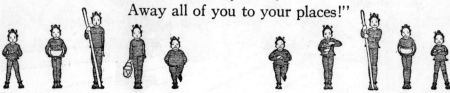

In the twinkling of an eye the little men popped into Elsa's fingers, and the old man vanished from sight. For a moment Elsa sat staring at her hands. Then suddenly a great desire to work came over her. Up she jumped.

"Why am I idling here?" she cried. "It is late in the morning and nothing done in the house!" And she hastened off to the kitchen. Soon she was giving orders to the servants, setting things to rights everywhere and singing while she prepared the dinner.

When Gunner came home that night, all was clean and bright to welcome him, and Elsa's face shone brighter than all the rest. "Oh, ho!" he cried heartily, "some good fairy has been here!"

Elsa smiled and held up her ten rosy fingers.

"Ten good fairies," she said.

After that Elsa rose early each morning, and went about her work sweet-tempered and happy. The farmhouse prospered under her hands, and health, wealth, and happiness came to stay when she learned how to manage those ten little elves.

49

The Selfish Giant*
OSCAR WILDE

EVERY afternoon, as they were coming from school, the children used to go and play in the Giant's garden. It was a large, lovely garden, with soft, green grass. Here and there over the grass stood beautiful flowers like stars. And there were twelve peach trees, that, in the spring-time, broke into delicate blossoms of pink and pearl and, in the autumn, bore rich fruit. The birds sat on the trees and sang so sweetly that the children used to stop their games in order to listen to them.

"How happy we are here!" they cried to each other.

One day the Giant came back. He had been to visit his friend, the Cornish ogre, and had stayed with him for seven years. After the seven years were over he had said all that he had to say, for his conversation was limited, and he determined to return to his own castle. When he arrived he saw the children playing in the garden.

*Taken from *Fairy Tales*. Used by the courteous permission of G. P. Putnam's Sons.

"What are you doing here?" he cried in a very gruff voice, and the children ran away.

"My own garden is my own garden," said the Giant, "anyone can understand that, and I will allow nobody to play in it but myself." So he built a high wall all around it, and put up a notice-board:

Trespassers Will Be Prosecuted

He was a very selfish Giant.

The poor children had now nowhere to play. They tried to play on the road, but the road was very dusty and full of hard stones, and they did not like it. They used to wander round the high wall when their lessons were over, and talk about the beautiful garden inside. "How happy we were there," they said to each other.

Then the Spring came; and all over the country, there were little blossoms and little birds. Only in the garden of the Selfish Giant, it was still winter.

51

The birds did not care to sing in it as there were no children, and the trees forgot to blossom. Once a beautiful flower put its head out from the grass, but, when it saw the notice-board, it was so sorry for the children that it slipped back into the ground again and went off to sleep. The only people who were pleased were the Snow and the Frost. "Spring has forgotten this garden," they cried, "so we will live here all the year round." The Snow covered up the grass with her white cloak, and the Frost painted all the trees silver. Then they invited the North Wind to stay with them, and he came. He was wrapped in furs, and he roared all day about the garden and blew the chimney pots down. "This is a delightful spot," he said, "we must ask the Hail on a visit." So the Hail came. Every day for three hours he rattled on the roof of the castle till he broke most of the slates, and then he ran round and round the garden as fast as he could go. He was dressed in grey, and his breath was like ice.

"I cannot understand why the Spring is so late in coming," said the Selfish Giant, as he sat at the window and looked out at his cold, white garden. "I hope there will be a change in the weather."

But the Spring never came, nor the Summer. The Autumn gave golden fruit to every garden, but, to the Giant's garden, she gave none. "He is too selfish," she said.

THROUGH THE GATE

So it was always Winter there, and the North Wind, and the Hail, and the Frost, and the Snow danced about through the trees.

One morning, the Giant was lying awake in bed when he heard some lovely music. It sounded so sweet to his ears that he thought it must be the King's musicians passing by. It was really only a little linnet singing outside his window, but it was so long since he had heard a bird sing in his garden that it seemed to him to be the most beautiful music in the world. Then the Hail stopped dancing over his head, and the North Wind ceased roaring, and a delicious perfume came to him through the open casement. "I believe the Spring has come at last," said the Giant; and he jumped out of bed and looked out. What did he see?

He saw a most wonderful sight. Through a little hole in the wall the children had crept in, and they were sitting in the branches of the trees. In every tree that he could see there was a little child. And the trees were so glad to have the children back again that

53

they had covered themselves with blossoms, and were waving their arms gently above the children's heads. The birds were flying about and twittering with delight, and the flowers were looking up through the green grass and laughing. It was a lovely scene, only in one corner it was still winter. It was the farthest corner of the garden, and in it was standing a little boy. He was so small that he could not reach up to the branches of the tree, and he was wandering all around it, crying bitterly. The poor tree was still quite covered with frost and snow, and the North Wind was blowing and roaring above it. "Climb up, little boy!" said the Tree, and bent its branches down as low as it could; but the boy was too tiny.

And the Giant's heart melted as he looked out. "How selfish I have been!" he said, "now I know why the Spring would not come here. I will put that poor little boy on the top of the tree, and then I will knock down the wall, and my garden shall be the children's playground for ever and ever."

He was really very sorry for what he had done.

So he crept downstairs and opened the front door quite softly, and went out into the garden. But when the children saw him they were so frightened that they all ran away, and the garden became winter again. Only the little boy did not run, for his eyes were so full of tears that he did not see the Giant coming. And the Giant stole up behind him and took him gently in his hand, and put him up into the tree. And the tree broke at once into blossom, and the birds came and sang on it, and the little boy stretched out his two arms and flung them around the Giant's neck and kissed him. And the other children when they saw that the Giant was not wicked any longer, came running back, and with them came the Spring. "It is your garden now, little children," said the Giant, and he took a great axe and knocked down the wall. And when the people were going to market at twelve o'clock, they found the Giant playing with the children in the most beautiful garden they had ever seen.

55

THE LITTLE TOY LAND OF THE DUTCH
Olive Beaupré Miller

AWAY, 'way off 'cross the seas and such
Lies the little flat land of the Dutch, Dutch, Dutch!

Where the green toy meadows stretch off to the sea,
With a little canal where a fence ought to be!

Where the windmills' arms go round, round, round,
And sing to the cows with a creaky sound,

Where storks live up in the chimney top,
And wooden shoes pound, plop, plop, plop!

Where little toy houses stand in a row,
And dogcarts clattering past them go!

Where milk cans shine in the shiniest way,
And the housemaids scrub, scrub, scrub all day.

Where dikes keep out the raging sea,
And shut in the land as cozy as can be.

Oh, that little toy land, I like it much,
That prim little, trim little, land of the Dutch!

THROUGH THE GATE

The Boy Hero of Harlem

A LEGEND OF HOLLAND

HANS, in his wooden shoes, ran clatter-ing along the brick pavement that ran beside a canal in the old Dutch city of Harlem. He was on his way to take some beautiful gingerbread cakes to a very dear friend of his, an old man who lived down by the sea. Swinging his basket and whistling, he hurried down the shady streets and out into the country. Soon he overtook a little girl who was driving a flock of geese.

"Look, boy!" cried the girl. "See how swollen with water the canal is! It is almost overflowing."

"Yes," answered Hans, "it is the spring rains that have done it. My father keeps the sluice gates. I'm glad his gates are big and strong, so he can shut out the sea, and keep the water from flooding the land."

The little girl, with the geese, shivered as he spoke. "Just suppose," said she, "that the sea should get through the gates or suppose it should break through the dikes! Where would Harlem be then?"

Neither child spoke for a moment. Each was think-ing how the mossy old windmills round about, and the black and white cows that grazed peacefully on the rich green meadows, and the neat little red-brick farm-houses, and the trim shade trees by the canal, and the whole city of Harlem would all be swept away if the

57

water got through the sluice gates, or through the great, thick, grass-grown mud embankment of the dikes; for Holland lay lower than the sea and nothing but those dikes kept the ocean from rushing in like some great, powerful monster to devour all the peaceful land.

"Don't be thinking of that, girl," Hans started to whistle again. "The dikes and the sluice gates are watched. They are watched so carefully that they could never give way, so Harlem is safe after all."

The children trudged on together. Sometimes they saw a sailboat that seemed to fly over the meadows, so hidden from sight was the tiny canal along which it was skimming; sometimes they passed by fields of the flaming, bright-colored tulips for which Harlem was famous; often they crossed little bridges over the canals.

At last Hans bade the goose-girl good-bye and went on his way alone. Soon he saw looming up the grassy wall of the sea-dike, with the little house of his friend nestled down beneath it. On a level with the roof of the house— yes, on a level with the roof—he saw the shining sea and the ships afloat on the water.

For a moment, he thought again how quickly the sea would rush in and cover all the land if once it could get through the dike. But the sun was shining peacefully and calmly overhead and the world seemed merry and safe, so he put the thought aside and went on into the house. His old friend was delighted with the beautiful ginger-bread cakes, and Hans sat in front of his cottage all through

the afternoon, while the old man mended his nets and told long and interesting tales of life on the sea.

When the boy started out for home, the sun was setting in the West. It was much later than he had thought and he must hurry now. Supper would be ready and his mother would be waiting. In order to return by the very shortest way, he took the road that ran along the top of the dike. The soft velvet dusk of twilight was settling over the earth, and a star had appeared in the sky, when, as he hurried on, he suddenly heard a faint gurgle. On the instant, he stopped; a gurgle meant water running through some little hole. Carefully Hans leaned down and peered over the embankment on the opposite side from the sea. Sure enough! There, in the dike, he saw a little chink and through it a small stream of water was trickling, trickling, trickling.

A leak in the dike! A leak in the dike! All the

meaning of those words flashed over the boy in a moment. Bit by bit, the water, running through that small opening, would wash away the earth and rocks of which the embankment was made. Thus it would make the hole larger till it swept through the dike altogether, and rolled down over the meadows, over the red-brick farmhouses, over the home of his family — down, down, down, over Harlem.

Hans hesitated not an instant. He slid to the bottom of the dike, and thrust his arm into the chink. Then he shouted loudly for help, but the place was lonely and no one heard him. He looked about to find something with which to stop up the hole while he should go for aid. There was no material near that was strong enough to hold back the water. His arm and his arm alone could keep out the rush of the waves. Well, he would keep it there until some one came along.

Loud boomed the sea in the darkness; the moon came out on the water and shed a track of silver over the bounding waves; but no one came up the dike and there were no answers to his calls.

"I am the great, great sea," the waters seemed to roar. "I can overwhelm all with my power. What can one boy do against me? I can overcome all!"

But the boy's heart grew strong within him. He would not be driven away. His hand grew cold and numb; his arm grew stiff to the shoulder, but still he did not falter. He thought of his mother and father and his little brother at home; he thought of the people sleeping so peacefully in Harlem; he thought of the very geese! And the safety of these, all these, depended on the faithfulness with which he kept that arm fixed fast in the little chink until in time help should come.

All night he listened for sounds, straining his ears to hear, but the stillness was unbroken save for the boom of the sea. The boy scarcely moved as he crouched there. Only now and again he changed the arm that he held in the hole. It seemed as though ages had passed when the first faint streaks of dawn began to appear in the sky. Lilac faded into rose, the gray sea sprang into life and sparkled with a million sparkles, when all at once he heard a faint noise in the distance. Nearer it came and nearer, till he saw coming toward him a dog-cart bearing a man and a boy and some shining bright copper milk cans. A milkman off for town to make his morning rounds—someone had come at last!

"Help! Here, help!" cried Hans faintly.

"Who cries help?" the man shouted.

"Here! Here!" answered Hans.

Then the milkman spied him and hurried to his side.

"In the name of all that is good, boy, what are you doing?" he cried.

"There's a leak in the dike," Hans answered. "I'm holding my arm in the hole to keep the water from running in. Go and bring help as soon as you can!"

In another moment, the lad was clattering off in the

dog-cart, going at full speed toward town, to report what
had happened to the dike. The man staying there with
Hans, helped the boy to stand on his feet and stretch his
stiffened limbs. Then he put his own arm into the hole
to keep the leak stopped up until his son should have
time to send them help from the city.

Soon a crowd of men appeared, hurrying out from
Harlem. And when they had mended the dike, they
took Hans up on their shoulders and bore him back to town.

"Make way for the hero of Harlem!" they cried as
they walked through the city. "Make way! Make
way for the boy who has saved you all from the sea!"

Christening the Baby in Russia*

ARTHUR RANSOME

SOMEWHERE in the forest of great trees is the hut where old Peter lives.

The hut was made of pine logs cut from the forest. You could see the marks of the axe. Old Peter was the grandfather of Maroosia and Vanya. He lived alone with them in the hut in the forest; and they were happy with old Peter, who was very kind to them and did all he could to keep them warm and well-fed.

Besides old Peter and Maroosia and Vanya, there were Vladimir and Bayan. Vladimir was a cat, a big black cat, as stately as an emperor, and just now he was lying in Vanya's arms fast asleep. Bayan was a dog, a tall, gray wolf dog. He could jump over the table with a single bound. When he was in the hut he usually lay underneath the table, because that was the only place where he could lie without being in the way. Just now he was out with old Peter.

Vladimir stirred suddenly in Vanya's lap; and a minute later, they heard the scrunch of boots. Then the door opened, and Bayan pushed his way in and shook himself, and licked Maroosia and Vanya and startled Vladimir, and lay down under the table and came out again, because he was so pleased to be home. And old Peter came in after him.

"You are snug in here, little pigeons," he said.

*From *Old Peter's Russian Tales*. Used by the courteous permission of Frederick A. Stokes Company.

63

Vanya and Maroosia had jumped up to welcome him and, when he opened his big sheepskin coat, they tumbled into it together and clung to his belt. Then he closed the big woolly coat over the top of them and they squealed; and he opened it a little way and looked down at them over his beard, and then closed it again before letting them out. He did this every night, and Bayan always barked when they were shut up inside.

Then old Peter took off his big coat and lifted down the samovar from the shelf. The samovar is like a big tea urn, with a red-hot fire in the middle of it keeping the water boiling. It hums like a bee on the tea-table, and the steam rises in a little jet from a tiny hole in the top. The boiling water comes out of a tap at the bottom. Old Peter threw in the lighted sticks and charcoal, and then set the samovar on the table with the little fire crackling in its inside. Then he cut some big lumps of black bread. Then he took a great saucepan full of soup, that was simmering on the stove, and emptied it into a big wooden bowl. Then he went to the wall where, on three nails, hung three wooden spoons—deep, like ladles. There was one big spoon, for old Peter; and two little spoons, one for Vanya and one for Maroosia.

And all the time that old Peter was getting supper ready, he was answering questions and making jokes—about what the Man in the Moon said when he fell out, and what the wolf said who caught his own tail and ate himself up before he found out his mistake.

And Vanya and Maroosia danced about the hut and chuckled. Then they had supper, all three dipping their wooden spoons in the big bowl together, and eating a tremendous lot of black bread. And, of course, there were scraps for Vladimir and a bone for Bayan.

Old Peter had a sister who lived in the village not so very far away from the forest. And she had a plump

Well-tuned to Russian joy in horses and picturesque vehicles is *Troika en Traineaux* by the Russian, Tchaikovsky, a musical description of a sleigh, with tinkling sleigh-bells, drawn over the snow by three horses harnessed abreast.

daughter, and the daughter was called Nastasia, and Nastasia was married to a handsome peasant called Sergie, who had three cows, a lot of pigs, and a flock of fat geese. And tonight old Peter said to the children, "There's something new in the village."

"What sort of a something?" asked Vanya.

"Alive," said old Peter.

"Is there a lot of it?" asked Vanya.

"No, only one."

"Then it can't be pigs," said Vanya.

"Perhaps it is a little calf," said Maroosia.

"I know what it is," said Vanya. "It's a foal. It's brown all over with white on its nose, and a lot of white hairs in its tail."

"No."

"What is it then, grandfather?"

"I'll tell you, little pigeons. It's small and red, and it's got a bumpy head with hair on it like the fluff of a duckling. It has blue eyes, and ten fingers to its fore paws, and ten toes to its hind feet—five to each."

"It's a baby," said Maroosia.

"Yes. Nastasia has got a little son; you have got a new cousin; and I have got a new grand-nephew."

"Who is going to the christening?" cried the children.

"The baby, of course."

"Yes; but other people?"

"All the village."

"And us?"

THROUGH THE GATE

"I have to go, and I suppose there'll be room in the cart for two little bear cubs like you."

And so it was settled that Vanya and Maroosia were to go to the christening of their new cousin. All the next day they could think of nothing else; and early on the morning of the christening, they were up and about, Maroosia seeing that Vanya had on a clean shirt, and herself putting a green ribbon in her hair. The sun shone, and the leaves on the trees were all new and bright, and the sky was pale blue through the flickering green leaves.

Old Peter was up early too, harnessing the little yellow horse to the old cart. The cart was of rough wood, without springs, like a big box fixed on long larch poles between two pairs of wheels. The larch poles did instead of springs, bending and creaking, as the cart moved over the forest track. The shafts came from the front wheels upward to the horse's shoulders; and between the ends of them, there was a tall, strong hoop of wood, called a douga, which rose high over the shoulders of the horse above his collar and had two little bells hanging from it at the top. The wooden hoop was painted blue with little yellow flowers. The harness was mostly ropes, but that did not matter so long as it held together. The horse had a long tail and mane, and looked as untidy as a little boy; but he had a green ribbon in his forelock in honour of the christening and he could go like anything and never got tired.

When all was ready, old Peter arranged a lot of soft fresh hay in the cart for the children to sit in. Hay is the best thing in the world to sit in when you drive in a jolting Russian cart. Old Peter put in a tremendous lot, so that the horse could eat some of it while waiting in the village and yet leave them enough to make them comfortable on the journey back.

68

THROUGH THE GATE

Presently Vanya and Maroosia were tucked into the hay, and old Peter climbed in with the plaited reins, and away they went along the narrow forest track, where the wheels followed the ruts and splashed through the deep holes; for the spring was young and the roads had not yet dried. Some of the deepest holes had a few pine branches laid in them, but that was the only road-mending that ever was done. Overhead were the tall firs and silver birches with their little, pale, round leaves; and somewhere, not far away, a cuckoo was calling, while the murmur of the wild pigeons never stopped for a moment.

They drove on and on through the forest, and at last came out from among the trees into the open country, a broad, flat plain stretching to the river.

Far away they could see the big, square sail of a boat, swelled out in the light wind, and they knew that there was the river, on the banks of which stood the village. They could see a small clump of trees, and, as they came nearer, the pale green cupolas of the white village church rising high up above the tops of the birches.

They passed a little girl with a flock of geese, and another little girl lying in the grass holding a long rope which was fastened to the horns of a brown cow. And the little girl lay on her face and slept among the flowers, while the cow walked slowly round her, step by step, chewing the grass and thinking about nothing at all.

And at last they came to the village, where the road was wider; and instead of one pair of ruts there were dozens, and the cart bumped worse than ever. The broad earthy road had no stones in it; and in places where the puddles would have been deeper than the axles of the wheels, it had been mended by laying down fir logs and small branches in the puddles, and putting a few spades full of earth on the top of them.

The road ran right through the village. On either side of it were little wooden huts. The ends of the timbers crossed outside at the four corners of the huts. They fitted neatly into each other, and some of them were carved. And there were thin slips of wood on the roofs over-lapping each other. There was not a single stone hut or cottage in the village. Only the church was partly brick, whitewashed, with bright green cupolas up in the air and thin gold crosses on the tops of the cupolas, shining in the clear sky.

Outside the church were rows of short posts, with long rough fir timbers nailed on the top of them, to which the country people tied their horses when they came to church. There were several carts there already, with bright-coloured rugs lying on the hay in them; and the horses were eating hay or biting the logs. Always, they bite the timbers, while their masters eat sun-flower seeds, not for food, but to pass the time.

"Now then," said old Peter, as he got down from the cart, tied the horse, gave him an armful of hay from the cart, and lifted the children out. "Be quick! We shall be late if we don't take care. I believe we are late already."

Old Peter hurried into the church, followed by Vanya and Maroosia. The ceremony was just beginning.

The priest, in his silk robes, was standing before the gold and painted screen at the end of the church; and there was the basin of holy water, and old Peter's sister, and the nurse Babka Tanya, very proud, holding the baby in a roll of white linen and rocking it to and fro. There were coloured pictures of saints all over the screen, which stretches from one side of the church to the other. Some of the pictures were framed in gilt frames under glass, and were partly painted and partly metal. The faces and hands of the saints were painted, and their clothes were glittering silver or gold. Little lamps and candles were burning in front of them.

A Russian christening is very different from an English one. For one thing, the baby goes right into the water, not once, but three times. Babka Tanya unrolled the baby, and the priest covered its face with his hand, and down it went under the water, once, twice, and again. Then he took some of the sacred ointment on his finger and anointed the baby's forehead, and feet, and hands, and little round stomach. Then, with a pair of scissors, he cut a little pinch of fluff from the baby's head, and rolled it into a pellet with the ointment, and threw the pellet into the holy water. And after that, the baby was carried solemnly three times 'round the holy water.

The priest blessed it and prayed for it; and there it was, a little true Russian, ready to be carried back to its mother, Nastasia, who lay at home in her cottage waiting for it.

When they got outside the church, they all went to Nastasia's cottage to congratulate her on her baby.

At last, toward evening, old Peter packed what was left of the hay into the cart, and packed Vanya and Maroosia in with the hay. Everybody said good-byes all around, and Peter climbed in and took up the rope reins. Vanya and Maroosia waved their hands, and off they drove, back again to the hut in the forest.

THROUGH THE GATE
The Little Snow Maiden*
A RUSSIAN FOLK TALE

ONCE there lived in a little village on the edge of a forest in Russia, a good man named Peter and his wife Anastasia. Now these two, though there was much merry company in the huts about them, were always sorrowing because they had no children in their home. The woman never had to run to her door and peep out to see that her little one did not wander away, because she had no little one. So Peter and Anastasia would stand at their window and watch the neighbor's children and wish with all their hearts that one of these was their own.

One day they saw the little ones in their sheepskin coats playing in the snow. The children made snow forts. They pelted each other with snowballs and laughed and shouted merrily. Then they rolled up the snow into a great snow woman; they put an old kerchief on her head and a little old shawl about her shoulders.

"Now, there's an idea, wife," said Peter. "Let us go out and make a little snow girl. Who knows but perhaps she will come alive and be a daughter to us!"

"Good!" says the wife. "It's worth trying at least."

So out went the two in their big coats and their fur hats, and there in the back yard where no one could see them, they set to work. They rolled the snow together and began to fashion it into a little maiden. And so long

*The ballet opera *The Snow Maiden* by the Russian composer, Rimski-Korsakov (1844-1908), although different in detail, is based on this old folk tale so characteristic of the Russian people. The music is typically Russian, portraying the vastness and strength of the country and the deep emotions of a people living where summer is short and winter long and hard.

73

had they tenderly dreamed of a little girl, that their great love fashioned her now a most beautiful creature—the loveliest ever seen. Well, toward evening, when the sky was opal and smoke color and the clouds lay purple on the edge of the earth, she was finished. There she stood before them, complete.

"Oh, my little white pigeon, speak to us!" says Peter.

"Run and skip like the other children!" says Anastasia.

Suddenly the little maid's eyelids began to quiver, a faint flush bloomed on her cheeks, her lips parted in a smile. Then her eyes opened, and lo! they were blue as the sky at noon! All at once, she skipped from her place and began dancing about in the snow, dancing like a little white sprite and laughing softly, dancing like snowflakes whirled in the wind.

"God be thanked," says Peter. "Now we have a little girl to live with us! Run, wife, and fetch a blanket to keep her warm!" So Anastasia ran and got a blanket and wrapped it about the little snow maid, and Peter picked her up and carried her into the house.

"You must not keep me too warm," she said. So Peter put her gently down on a bench farthest from the stove, and she smiled up at him and blew him a kiss. Then Anastasia got her a little white fur coat, and Peter went to the neighbor's and bought her a white fur cap and a pair of little white boots with white fur around the tops.

But, when she was dressed, the little snow maiden cried,

THROUGH THE GATE

"It is too hot in the cottage. I must go out in the cold."

"Nay, nay, my little pigeon," says Anastasia, "it is time I tucked you up all warm and cozy in a nice little bed."

"Oh, ho! No, no!" says the little snow maiden, "I am a little daughter of the Snow. I cannot be tucked up under a blanket. I will play by myself in the yard all night." And out she danced into the cold.

Over the gleaming snow she tripped, down the silver path of the moonlight.

Her garments glittered like diamonds, and the frost shone about her head like a little crown of stars.

For a long time the man and his good wife watched her.

"Ah, God be thanked for the little girl that has come to us," they said again and again. Then at last they went to bed, but more than once that night they rose to look out of the window and make sure she had not run away. There she was just as before, dancing about in the moonlight and playing all alone.

In the morning she ran into the cottage and her eyes were shining and glistening.

"This is the porridge for me," she cried, and she showed the good woman how to crush up a little piece of ice in a wooden bowl, for that was all she would eat.

After breakfast she ran out into the road and joined the other children at play. How she played and how the children loved her! She could run faster than all the rest. Her little white boots twinkled and gleamed as she ran; and, when she laughed, it was like the ringing peals of tiny silver bells.

The man and the woman watched her proudly.

"She is all our own," said Anastasia.

"Our little white pigeon," said Peter.

When it was time, she came in for her ice porridge. But, though Anastasia said to her, "To-night you'll surely sleep inside, my darling," she answered just as she had before, "Oh, ho! No, no! I'm a little daughter of the Snow!"

THROUGH THE GATE

Thus it went all through the winter. The little snow maiden made Peter and Anastasia very happy. She was forever singing and laughing and dancing in-and-out of the house, in-and-out of the house. She was very good, too, and she did everything Anastasia told her. Only she would never sleep indoors. She seemed happiest and most at home when the little snow-flakes were dancing about in the air, and no storm was ever too severe to seem other than her playfellow.

But, when there began to be signs of spring in the air, when the snow melted and one could run down the paths in the forest, when the tiny green shoots peeped up here and there, then the little snow girl seemed to be drooping and longing for something.

One day she came to Peter and Anastasia and said:

"Time has come when I must go
To my friends of Frost and Snow.
Good-bye, dear ones here, good-bye.
Back I go across the sky!"

Peter and Anastasia began to weep and lament very loudly. They wished to keep her all to themselves and share her with no one else.

"Ah, my darling, you must not go!" cried Peter.

"Ah, my darling, you shall not go!" cried Anastasia.

And Peter ran and barred the door while Anastasia put her arms about her darling and held her close up beside the stove.

"You shall not leave us! You shall not leave us!" they

77

cried. But even as Anastasia held her tight, she seemed to melt slowly away. At last there was nothing left but a pool of water by the stove with a little fur cap in the midst and a little fur coat and a pair of white boots. Yet it seemed to Anastasia and Peter as though they saw her still before them with her bright eyes shining, her long hair streaming, and they still seemed to hear her singing, faintly, very faintly:

> *"Time has come when I must go,*
> *To my friends of Frost and Snow.*
> *Good-bye, dear ones here, good-bye.*
> *Back I go across the sky!"*

"Oh, stay, stay, stay!" they begged, but all at once the very door that Peter had barred burst open. A cold wind swept into the room; and, when Peter had pushed the door shut again, lo! the little snow maiden had vanished!

Then Peter and Anastasia wept and thought they should never see her again. Anastasia carefully laid away the garments she had left behind; and often through the summer, she took out the little fur cap, the fur coat and the boots to kiss them and think of her darling. But, when winter had come again, it happened one starlit night that the two heard a silvery peal of laughter just outside the window.

"That sounds like our little snow maid!" cried Peter, and off he hurried to open the door. Sure enough! Into the room she danced, her eyes shining as she sang:

THROUGH THE GATE

"By frosty night and frosty day,
Your love calls me here to stay,
Here till Spring I stay and then
Back to Frost and Snow again!"

So Peter and Anastasia clasped the little snow maid in their arms; she put on her pretty white clothes again, and soon there she was out on the gleaming snow, tripping down the silver path of the moonlight, her garments glittering like diamonds, and the frost about her head like a crown of shining stars.

Each Springtime, off she went northward to play through the summer with her friends on the frozen seas; but every winter, she stayed in Russia with Peter and Anastasia and they came not to mind her going for they knew she would come again.

THE BIRCHES*

WALTER PRITCHARD EATON

The little birches, white and slim,
Gleaming in the forest dim,
Must think the day is almost gone,
For each one has her nightie on.

*From *Echoes and Realities*, copyright, 1918, George H. Doran Company, publishers.

A Thanksgiving Day from The Bible

LONG ago the Children of Israel served at hard labor in the brickyards of Egypt. Pharaoh, the King of Egypt, set taskmasters over them and they toiled as slaves in the burning sun. Then, there rose a man from among them, Moses by name, and he led the Children of Israel out of Egypt and through the desert to a land which God had promised unto them. And the Children of Israel settled in the Promised Land and were happy again. They built towns and vineyards, and the terraces of their hillsides waxed green with budding wheat. And when, in the autumn, they gathered the rich harvest into their storehouses, their hearts went out in thanksgiving to God who made all that was made and caused it to grow abundantly and give forth fruit for their use.

THROUGH THE GATE

And in honor of God, who had saved them from the wilderness and given them so rich a harvest, they kept, year after year, a solemn feast. The people took olive branches and pine branches and palm branches and they made themselves booths, everyone on the roof of his house and in their courts and in the streets. And they dwelt, not in their houses, but in the booths for seven days. And they rejoiced in the feast, they and their sons and their daughters and their manservants and their maidservants and the stranger and the fatherless that were within their gates.

Seven days they kept a solemn feast unto the Lord, because the Lord had blessed them in all their increase and in all the works of their hands. And they sang:

"O come, let us sing unto the Lord;
   Let us come before His presence with thanksgiving,
    And make a joyful noise unto Him with psalms.
Thou visitest the earth and waterest it;
   Thou greatly enrichest it with the river of God,
    Which is full of water;
     Thou preparest them corn
      When thou hast so provided for it.
Thou crownest the year with thy goodness:
   And thy paths drop fatness;
    They drop upon the pastures of the wilderness,
    And the little hills rejoice on every side.
  The pastures are clothed with flocks;
    The valleys also are covered over with corn;
     They shout for joy, they also sing!"

81

WHO CAN CRACK NUTS?*

Mary Mapes Dodge

Rut-a-tut-tuts!
Who can crack nuts?
Squirrels, can you?
"That we can, true—
Rut-a-tut-tuts,
We can crack nuts!"
Chicketty-chack,
Cracketty-crack,
"Pooh!" said the hammer,
"Silence your clamor,
Rut-a-tut-tuts—
Who can't crack nuts?"

*From *Rhymes and Jingles;* copyright, 1874, by Scribner, Armstrong & Co.; 1904, by Charles Scribner's Sons. By permission of the publishers.

The Nutcracker and Sugardolly Stories*
CAROLYN SHERWIN BAILEY

I

Once upon a time there were an old peddler and his wife going to town to market, and the peddler had a bag full of all sorts of nuts, and the woman had a basket of eggs upon her head.

The day was warm and sunny, and because the high road was so hot, they decided to go through the woods, a new way. As they went, they came to a beautiful shady path under the trees, a path they had never traveled before. On and on it went, until it ended all at once at a wonderful garden—a garden with a silver fence and a gold lattice gate all set with jewels, and over the gate was written a name in letters, "The Fairy Honeymouth."

*From *Firelight Stories*. Used by the permission of Milton Bradley Company.

The lattice gate was tightly closed, but behind it one could see gay flowers, and hear beautiful birds singing loudly in trees all made of sugar. On either side of the gate stood a great tree, and one tree bore large green nuts, nuts as large as hen's eggs, and the other was a sugar tree, dropping sugar plums down upon the path below.

"We must go inside," said the peddler, dropping his nuts. "We must indeed," said his wife, setting down her eggs. So they both climbed the lattice gate, and dropped down on the other side, although the birds in the garden sang loudly to them, "Don't do it. Don't do it."

Then the two buried their hands in the white sugar that filled the garden walks and smelled of the flowers that were all made of sugar, and at last the peddler said, "I must have one of those great green nuts. It would sell for more at the market than all the nuts I can gather in a twelve-month."

"Don't do it. Don't do it," called the birds, but the peddler paid no attention to them. He climbed the tree beside the gate and put one of the great green nuts in his pocket.

"See what I have found," called his wife, who had climbed the sugar tree. There in a nest lay a huge white egg.

"We will put this egg under our hen whose nest is beneath the front stairs. It will hatch into a wonderful fowl which we will sell for much money."

"Don't do it. Don't do it," sang the birds, but the woman took the large egg.

Then the two climbed the gate again and went away from the garden of the Fairy Honeymouth, carrying with them her great white egg, and one of her great green nuts, which, of course, they should never have done. When they reached home, they put the egg under their hen who had her nest beneath the front stairs, and the peddler laid the great green nut upon the table and got out his hammer, because he had decided to crack it.

Bang, bang, he pounded. The nutshell fell apart, but instead of a kernel inside, there on the table stood a strange little dwarf no bigger than your hand. He wore a wig, and yellow trousers and a hussar's jacket, with big buttons, quite tidy and complete. He had a huge head, and thin legs, and such a wide mouth that it seemed as if his head would come in two. He stepped out of the nutshell, and yawned, and, jumping into a basket of nuts, he began cracking them as fast as he could with his teeth.

But while this was happening, there came a great cackling from under the front stairs where the hen had her nest. The great white egg had hatched and out of it, upon the floor, hopped the daintiest little girl. She wore little silk skirts, and hose, and dancing shoes. Her hair was all curled in rings, and she picked up her petticoat and began whirling and dancing all

around the room. The hen went out to the barn-yard in a tiff, because she had hatched no chick, but the peddler and his wife looked in wonder at the little dwarf, cracking nuts with his huge mouth, and the little lady in her dancing shoes, flying about the floor. Then they whispered together, and they said:

"We have no children. We will keep these little ones, and they shall be our children, and we will name them Nutcracker and Sugardolly."

So that is how Nutcracker and Sugardolly came in the first place and lived with the peddler and his wife.

II

The peddler soon found that he had a very bad bargain. Nutcracker was a naughty little dwarf. All day long he did no good to anyone—only mischief. He got into the nuts that were ready to go to market, and he cracked every one with his great mouth. Then he climbed the nut trees outside, and threw shells at the people passing by. When the peddler's wife tried to catch him with her broom, out from under it he would slide, and jump to the shelf and hide inside the clock, or he would dance a little way ahead of the broom and make faces at the peddler's wife.

He had only two friends—the great big barnyard cock who took him for rides about the garden, and little Sugardolly whom he loved very dearly.

Now Sugardolly was almost as much trouble as Nutcracker, for she would do no work, and she could eat nothing but honey and sweets from the flowers; and if she could not have all the flowers in the garden she would sit in a corner and cry. It was Nutcracker who brought her sweets, and Nutcracker who comforted her when she cried. But at last, when Nutcracker had eaten all the nuts that were gathered in the house, and

all that grew in the garden, he decided to run away, for the peddler's house no longer amused him. So early one morning he buttoned his little soldier jacket tightly about him, hopped on the cock's back, the cock spread his wings, and they went over the wall and far, far away. Nutcracker had decided to make a home for Sugardolly somewhere else.

III

The old peddler awoke in the morning, and he found the house very, very still. No cock in the garden crowed, and no little dwarf Nutcracker was about, rattling nuts. And Sugardolly sat in a corner and cried all day long, nor would she be comforted by all the sweets in the garden, because Nutcracker had gone away. The old peddler took Sugardolly upon his knee, and got down the sugar bowl for her to eat from, but she still cried. For many, many days she sat in the chimney corner, and grew more and more thin.

At last the white hen, who had a nest beneath the front stairs, took pity on Sugardolly, and told her that Nutcracker had gone away on the cock's back.

"Oh, take me away, too," cried poor little Sugardolly. So the white hen, with Sugardolly on her back, early one morning flew over the garden wall and across the meadow to find Nutcracker.

At first they were not sure which way to go. No one had seen Nutcracker and the cock. But one day they found one of the cock's red tail feathers by the roadside, and a bit farther on they came to another, and then, when they had entered a deep, deep wood, they came to the cock himself, strutting proudly about, and gathering hazel nuts.

"Where, oh, where is my dear Nutcracker?" asked Sugardolly of the cock.

"That I do not know," said the cock. "He climbed a great tree, and that was the last I saw of him."

And when the white hen saw the cock, she decided to go no farther; so Sugardolly went on by herself to hunt for Nutcracker.

The woods were very dark when it came night, but Sugardolly carried a bright glow-worm for a lantern. In the morning she was asked to breakfast by some bees, who fed her all the honey she could eat.

"Have you seen Nutcracker—a little dwarf in a brown soldier's jacket?" she asked of the bees.

Oh, yes the bees had seen Nutcracker, but it had been many days before that he had passed by.

> "Buzz, buzz, buzz, buzz,
> Over grasses and flowers,
> Nutcracker has gone
> Through the wood's green bowers,"

hummed the bees, so Sugardolly hurried on.

She called to the birds as she went, "Have you seen my Nutcracker—a little dwarf with thin legs, and a very wide mouth?" And the birds sang back to Sugardolly:

"Pick, pick, pick, pick,
Be quick, be quick,
Yonder Nutcracker springs,
And rushes and rushes
Through the green bushes,
Be quick, be quick."

Sugardolly did hear a rustling, but when she crept beneath the bushes to see, she found only a squirrel who chattered and threw shells in her face.

Poor little Sugardolly! She called to the bluebells:

"Little bell flowers so blue,
Did Nutcracker pass you?"

But the wind shook the bluebells, and they answered not a word.

Sugardolly would have cried then, if she had not come, all at once, upon the fairy palace of the Queen Rosebush. The palace was made of green leaves, with thorns at the corners to keep out the crickets, and there came a sound of music and singing from inside.

"Is it a party?" asked Sugardolly of a gold bug.

"It is a party," said the gold bug. "I will take you in."

So Sugardolly went inside the palace with the gold bug and she saw the Queen in a rose-leaf dress and a veil of spider's net, sitting upon the throne, and the young princesses in bright, shining, golden dresses, sitting beside her. The birds were the orchestra.

"You may spend the night with us," said Queen Rosebush graciously.

THROUGH THE GATE

So Sugardolly slept in a pink rosebud all night, and breakfasted from ambrosia in the morning, and thanked the Queen for her kindness and started once more to look for Nutcracker.

As she went on her way through the forest, she came to a singing brook, and she sat down beside it to rest. And she listened, for the brook was singing to her as it flowed along its pebbles:

"From mountains I come,
Where the dwarfs have their home.
In the cave whence I spring,
Nutcracker is King.
To him swiftly flee;
His queen thou shalt be."

"I shall find my Nutcracker! I shall find my Nut-cracker!" said Sugardolly, jumping up. She ran and ran by the edge of the brook far, far along, as far as the brook flowed, calling, "Nutcracker, Nutcracker," but no Nutcracker answered.

At last she came to the place where the brook started from a deep cave, and as she called, "Nutcracker," the rocks answered back, "Nutcracker," and that was all—no little dwarf came out. So Sugardolly sat down on the rocks, very much discouraged, and tired, and after a while she fell fast asleep.

IV

I do not know how long Sugardolly slept by the cave where the brook started, but when she awoke, there at her side, underneath a water plant, sat a little brown dwarf, busily fishing for pearls. He looked very much like Nutcracker, except for his mouth, which was smaller, and his jacket, which was green instead of red.

"Good-day, little lady," said the dwarf to Sugardolly, and Sugardolly, who was a polite little lady, said "Good-day" in reply. Then the dwarf rolled up his net, and put his pearls in the little sack that hung by his side, and blew a shrill blast upon his tiny silver trumpet.

Out from all the cracks and crevices of the rocks came other, and still other little dwarfs, and they joined hands and danced about Sugardolly, and told her what a pretty little lady she was, and they asked her to be their queen.

"Have you seen my Nutcracker—a little dwarf in yellow trousers?" asked Sugardolly.

Then all the dwarfs began shaking their little fists and stamping their little feet, and scowling in a terrible rage.

"Nutcracker was a wicked king," said one of the dwarfs.

"He ate all of our nuts that we had gathered for the winter," said another.

"He stole our bag of gold nuts," said a third, "and he threw them into the brook because he broke his tooth trying to crack one."

"We drove him away from our home," said the first dwarf.

Then Sugardolly began to cry, but the dwarfs forgot their rage to see her so unhappy. They brought her a tiny scepter, and a glittering crown all set with jewels, so Sugardolly decided to be their queen.

And Sugardolly was happier than she had been in a long time. The dwarfs found a fairy baker who brought her every morning jars of honey, and sugar rolls, and sweet, sweet cakes in his basket—all she could eat. The dwarfs made a set of tiny furniture for her, a bed and a chair and a table of sea shells, inlaid with real gold.

And while the dwarfs were away all day at their work, creeping into the cracks and holes of the earth for gold and silver and jewels, Sugardolly did their housekeeping. She dusted, and polished their dishes, and made their beds, and she always had their tea brewed

when they came home with their stores. One day she found their gold nuts in the brook, which made them very happy. Then, at night, the dwarfs sat about their fire, crosslegged on the floor, warming their toes, and they sang songs to Sugardolly upon her throne, and they told her stories. So, after a while, Sugardolly forgot to be lonely for Nutcracker, and she was very happy indeed, being queen of the dwarfs.

V

Now all this time Nutcracker was lost in the deep, deep woods. He had been most ungrateful, and he had hidden himself in a tree because he wished all the nuts of the forest for his own little self, and he wanted the cock, who had been so very kind to him, to go home again. So the cock did go home, as you know, with the white hen, after eating a great many hazel nuts, and selfish little Nutcracker was left alone with all the forest to wander about in.

For a while in the sunny, pleasant weather, Nutcracker had a good time. He climbed all the trees, and sampled all the different sorts of nuts. Never before had he been able to eat all the nuts he wanted, so he cracked hazel nuts, and walnuts, and butternuts, and filberts, and he made a pile of empty shells as high as a berry bush; but alas, the frosts came!

Nutcracker's jacket and his yellow trousers were not warm enough for the chill nights and the keen, frosty mornings. He longed for the peddler's kitchen and the warm porcelain stove. He wished to hide himself beneath the cock's wings or creep into the nest of the white hen under the front stairs, but none of these things could Nutcracker do, for he had forgotten the way home.

At the foot of a large oak tree lived a great red

squirrel, who was chief of all the squirrels in the woods. It was he who divided the forest into parts, and every squirrel had his own trees and his own holes in which to live. The red squirrel walked out often to see that no other squirrel gathered the nuts which belonged to his neighbor, and he had a fine fur great-coat which he wore to keep himself warm.

Now Nutcracker had seen the red squirrel, and had admired his fur coat, and had thrown nut shells at him; and one night Nutcracker went stealthily to the oak tree where the chief squirrel lived and he stole the fur coat while the squirrel was sleeping.

It exactly fitted Nutcracker, and he turned up the collar and danced about quite gayly. But the chief squirrel awoke and missed his coat. In a rage he sent word to all the squirrels of the forest to rise and make war upon Nutcracker, which they did.

They followed Nutcracker wherever he went, and took away his nuts. His sword, that was no bigger than a cambric needle, was of no avail to drive them away. He was obliged to hide under the dry leaves, and he grew very, very thin. One day, as he sat shivering and hungry, he heard a sound of feet and a crunching upon the leaves. A great four-legged creature nearly stepped upon him, and as he cried out, a boy, whose dog it was that had frightened him, came along, and Nutcracker told him all his troubles.

"You shall go home with me," said the boy. "We

have a nut tree in the garden and you shall live in the chimney corner and be my playfellow." So Nutcracker went home with the boy and the dog, and his troubles were over for a while at least.

VI

Every evening Sugardolly, Queen of the Dwarfs, counted the little men, as they sat about the fire, to see if they had all come home, and one night a little dwarf was missing. So Sugardolly counted them all over again—one, two, three; yes, one was certainly missing. Then all the other dwarfs ran about crying, and wringing their hands, and looking under the beds and beneath the tables, and, as they looked, the door opened and in ran the little lost dwarf, very much out of breath and tired.

He had a bundle of moss upon his back, which he dropped upon the floor, and he told them all how he had been gathering the moss from a castle hedge, and how he had been attacked by a cat which charged him from the castle kitchen, and the cat was driven by none other than Nutcracker, their old king.

"Oh," cried Sugardolly, "may I not go to the castle? May I not see my dear Nutcracker? I have been your queen for a long time. May I not be released?"

So the dwarfs saw that Sugardolly would be no longer happy with them, in spite of the honey, the gold furniture, and the stories, so they bowed their heads sadly and said, "Yes," to her.

"But you must not go alone," they said, "we will take you as far as the castle hedge, and guard you from the cat and leave you there, Sugardolly."

So, early in the morning, a wonderful procession set out for the castle. At the head marched the dwarf who knew the way to the place where Nutcracker had been seen. Behind, marched three other dwarfs, carrying Sugardolly on their shoulders, and last of all came the rest of the dwarfs with their swords at their sides, ready to attack the fierce cat.

But they did not meet the cat, and they reached the lodge in safety. There they set Sugardolly down, very carefully, and said, "Good-by," to her very sadly, for they were sorry indeed to lose their queen.

Then Sugardolly crept under the castle hedge, and hurried across the garden to the kitchen, and tried the kitchen door, but it was locked. So she went in the cellar window, and climbed the cellar stairs, and many more stairs, until she found herself in a great warm room. There was a wide fireplace, and a white bed where a little girl lay fast asleep, as it was still early morning. In the corner of the room there rose a little figure, wearing a hussar's jacket and having a huge and wide mouth.

"Ah, my dear Nutcracker," said Sugardolly, running over to him, with her arms spread wide.

"My dear little Sugardolly," cried Nutcracker, taking her tenderly in his arms.

Just then the little girl awoke, and sat up in bed, and rubbed her eyes to see the little lady in her silk skirts and dancing shoes. Sugardolly began to dance for joy, and the little girl clapped her hands.

"Such a tiny, pretty little thing," said the little girl. "You shall live with us, and be my doll."

So that is how Sugardolly found Nutcracker.

VII

The castle children loved Sugardolly dearly. She sang them all the songs she had learned from the bees, and the birds, and the gold bugs. She told them about the party at the palace of the Fairy Rosebush, and her housekeeping in the cave of the dwarfs.

And Nutcracker, for once in his life, was useful. He was able to climb up to the high places in the garden and fetch down the toys when they were lost—the hoop, the ball, and the shuttlecock. So the children fed

Nutcracker all the nuts he could eat, and Sugardolly all the sugar she wished, and matters went very well for a while. But, after a little, the time drew near to Christmas. In the corner cupboard of the castle play-room there was a mouse hole, and through the mouse hole for weeks before Christmas came the Fairy Honey-mouth, bringing chains of sugar corn, and silver cobwebs, and gold nuts for the Christmas tree.

Now, the castle children never opened the door of the corner cupboard, for they knew that they should not. But Nutcracker and Sugardolly grew very curious, and, because they had not good manners, one night, when the whole castle was asleep, they opened the door. They saw the gold nuts and the silver cobwebs, and they found the mouse hole.

"Let us go through this dark passage," said Nut-cracker, "and see where it ends."

So the two squeezed themselves through the mouse hole and hurried along until they reached the end of the passage. And there they found themselves in the most beautiful place—the garden of their god-mother, the Fairy Honeymouth. There was the same silver fence, and the gold lattice gate, the tree with the great green nuts on one side, and the sugar tree on the other, the birds singing, and sugar, sugar everywhere.

They forgot all about the castle children who had been so kind to them. Nutcracker began pulling out the birds' tail feathers to stick in his cap. He climbed the trees, and shook down all the nuts. Sugardolly filled her pockets and her shoes with sugar, and began tearing up by their roots the sugar flowers.

"Don't do it. Don't do it," sang the birds sadly, as they had sung once before to the peddler and his wife, but Nutcracker and Sugardolly did not heed them. They went on spoiling the garden.

Then, out of her palace in a rage came their godmother, the Fairy Honeymouth.

"Naughty Nutcracker, naughty Sugardolly, to run away so often," said the Fairy Honeymouth. She touched them with her wand. "You," she said to Nutcracker, "shall be turned to wood, and crack nuts all your life, but never eat another." And to Sugardolly she said, "You shall be turned to a sugar doll." And that is what happened to Nutcracker and Sugardolly.

Upon Christmas morning the castle children opened the door of the corner cupboard. Oh, the wonder of it! All the old toys were gone, and new ones stood in their places. In glittering splendor stood the Christmas tree hung with sugar chains, and silver cobwebs and gold nuts. And listen! On the tip top of the tree stood Sugardolly, her hair still curled, her skirts still outspread, and she was still wearing her dancing shoes, but her hair, and her skirts, and her shoes were made of pink sugar. And beneath Sugardolly, his great head peering out from the branches, his jacket tidily buttoned, and his wide mouth open, ready to crack the Christmas nuts that he might never eat, hung Nut-cracker, all made of wood.

The news reached the cock who lived in the ped-dler's barnyard, and he mounted to the highest church steeple in town to try to see what had become of his old friend Nutcracker. And the cock stands there still, blown by all the winds of heaven, for he was not able to climb down again. And when the nights are chill and frost flies, when the storms beat against the window-pane, little children sit by the fire and tell the true stories of Nutcracker and Sugardolly, who had so many adventures, and who will hang on the Christmas tree as long as children believe in fairies.

A CHILD IN A MEXICAN GARDEN*
GRACE H. CONKLING

My garden-ground is very green,
With little streaks of light between,
And walls all made of white and red
Hold up the sky above my head.

I think sometimes that walls so high
Will never let the clouds get by;
But always, somehow and at last,
Over they slide and travel past.

*Taken from *Everybody's Magazine*.

103

The Battle of the Frogs and Mice*
RETOLD FROM A CLASSIC GREEK POEM

HARK, while I sing of that dread war between the Mice and Frogs, which caused the heavens to shake as in the days when giants strove on earth.

Once upon a time, a gentle mouse, all out of breath and tired with fleeing from a monstrous cat, dropped down to cool his thirst, and dipped his whiskers in a little pool. Thereat, a frog from out the water popped his head and hoarsely cried:

"Who are you, stranger, and why have you come hither panting for your breath? If you will tell me truly, you shall find in me a friend. I'll grant you entrance to the pleasures of this lake and you shall wander o'er my palace grounds and feast with me. This silver kingdom of the Pool and all the frogs obey me as their King. Great Swell-the-cheeks am I. My father was King Mud. And you, your form and manner, make me know that you, too, are a King, son of some warrior-hero. Tell me who you are."

The frog thus ceased to speak and thus the mouse replied: "My name is known to beasts and men and all

*In this amusing imitation of the great Greek war epic, the *Iliad*, mice and frogs act just like classic warriors. For years the poem was believed to have been written by Homer, the author of the *Iliad*, but is now thought to have been written a century or so after his time.

the birds that fly. Prince Steal-the-grain am I. My father is King Nibbler-of-the-bread. But now, since you and I are both so different in our natures, how can we be friends? No cheese, nor honey cake, nor gilded bacon, nay, nor bread, can hide itself from me. But stalks and water herbs and all that frogs delight to eat, have no delights for me. Such food no mouse of any taste can bear. And so, farewell."

The downy Prince thus spoke his mind, but still the croaking King did urge:

"Fair stranger, you speak well, yet know that we, the frogs, not only sport in water, but likewise dance on land, and in both places gather food. So trust yourself to make a visit to my kingdom. I myself will bear you through the waters. Only jump up on my shoulders, and I swear that you shall safely reach my marshy court."

He spoke and leaned his back in readiness. Thereon, the mouse, persuaded, lightly leapt with nimble bound, and round the Frog King's neck he clasped his arms. Now, wondering, he glides away and gladly looks about to see the sights on every side. But O alack, when curling waves begin to rise and wet his downy sides, his thoughts grow sad and full of woe. How then he sorrows for the shore! Alack, he cannot swim! His tears flow down; he tears his hair and lifts his trembling feet above the water's angry roll. He sighs and trails his tail behind him in the waves, an oar with which he tries in vain to steady his wild plunging boat.

And as he sorrowed thus, lo, from the deep a hissing water snake arose, to roll his bloodshot eyes and dart with active rage along the surface of the pond. The Frog King now beheld that snake, and, all confused at such a sight, he dived to hide himself beneath the waves. Forgetful frog! He took no thought for that new friend whom he was bearing on his back, but pitched him head-long in the deep. Unskilled in swimming and so far from shore, the princely Mouse flings out his arms in vain. He, plunging, sinks and, struggling, mounts again, and sinks and strives, but strives in vain. And these last words from his pale lips resound:

"O traitor, traitor-frog! To fling me floundering from your back! Ye mice, arise and punish this false foe!"

This said, he sank to rise no more.

But now it chanced a gallant mouse, young Lick-the-dish, was loitering on the flowery bank and basking idly in

the sun's bright beams. He sees Prince Steal-the-grain
go down and shrieks aloud. The shores re-echo to his
cries, and thus the Nibbling Nation learns the fate that
has befallen him, their hero-prince. Sad, sorry grief is
now in every mouse's heart.   Deep murmurs sound. From
lodge to lodge the sacred heralds run, and summon all
to come at sunrise to the council where in glory reigns
great Nibbler-of-the-bread, their King.

When rosy-fingered morn had tinged the clouds, the
Nation gathered round about their King. Slow he arose
and spoke with heaving breast: "For our lost prince
the father's tears are mine, but public grief is yours.
Plunged in the lake by Swell-the-cheeks, he drowned.
Rouse all our mice to war, my friends. To arms! To arms!"

His words awake a fire in every breast.   The mice

begin to arm. The empty hulls of peas for buskins on their legs they bind, large shells of nuts for helmets on their heads. 'Tis needles that for lances serve the throng. They seize their shields, and so they stalk across the plain, while sunlight glints from all their points of steel. Dreadful in arms the marching mice appear.

And now the wondering frogs perceive a tumult near, and, leaping from the waters, form a ring to hearken whence the noises come. Too soon they see the marching crowd of mice, and there advancing to the fore, the valiant chief, Sir Creeper-into-pots, who bears the sacred herald's scepter in his hand, and thus he speaks:

"Ye frogs, we mice advance to punish your foul crime, for by the hand of Swell-the-cheeks, your King, our hapless Prince was slain. See there all decked in armor how we shake the shining lance! Then arm your host, the doubtful battle try, lead forth those frogs that have the soul to die!"

The chief draws back; the frogs the challenge hear, and, proudly swelling, much resent. Yet still they blame their King who by his thoughtless deed has brought this danger on their heads; but he, unwilling to admit his coward's act, now rising, speaks to clear his name with lies.

"O friends," he cries with false, deceiving tears, "I'm not to blame because their Prince lies drowned beneath the wave. He was a vain, conceited youth who tried our art of swimming out of pride, and being all unable to perform the feat, he sank. It was his fault alone that he was drowned. But now his people shower their anger on my guiltless head. Come, we will turn this war to victory, for I am innocent of any wrong. Now by the water's edge in armor bright we will await the battle shock. Bright shall the waters flash; loud shall the shores resound in honor of the victory of the frogs!"

His warriors hear and take his lies for truth, and so decide to offer battle to the mice.

Green is the suit his arming heroes choose; their glossy helmets are of shells, and tapering sea-reeds form their polished spears. Thus, dressed for war, they take the appointed height.

> *Now front to front the marching armies shine,
> Halt e'er they meet and form the lengthening line;
> The chiefs conspicuous seen and heard afar,
> Give the loud sign to loose the rushing war.
> Their dreadful trumpets, deep-mouthed hornets sound.
> The sounded charge remurmurs o'er the ground.

First to the fight, Loud-brawler-frog now flies, and with his spear he slays brave Lick-stick who with generous flame stands forth before his comrades in the mousy line. The luckless warrior of the mice with javelin in breast, falls thundering to the ground. Alack! all soiled in dust his lovely tresses lie!

Now Scamper-into-holes has pierced the great frog hero, Stick-in-mud, a dreadful stroke that strikes dark fear straight to the heart of Cabbage-eater-frog. In head-long flight doth Cabbage-eater run, a frog long used to feasts and dainty fare, but less prepared for trials of pluck

*From Parnell's Translation.

and skill. In headlong flight he runs, and, stumbling
o'er the brink, falls in the lake.

And now that mighty mouse, great Robber-of-the-gran-
aries, in glory shines afar. At sight of him the mighty
Croaker, Prince of Frogs, takes from the lake a monstrous
mass of mud to hurl it at his foe. The cloud of dirt falls
showering o'er the warrior mouse, dishonoring his face and
blinding his bright eyes. Enraged and wildly spluttering,
from the shore the hero Robber grasps a stone immense
of size, a stone so great that but to lift its weight would
take ten weak, degenerate mice of modern days. He hurls
the stone upon his foe and strikes him down.

> Then nobly towering o'er the rest, appears
> A gallant prince, far taller than his years,
> His father's pride, the glory of his house,
> And more a Mars in battle than a mouse,
> His action bold, and strong his powerful frame,
> And Mer-i-dar'-pax his resounding name.
> This warrior, standing forth from out the crowd,
> Boasts the dire honors of his arms aloud;
> Then, strutting near the lake, with looks elate,
> Threats all its nations with approaching fate.

Ah, then it seemed as though the mice would make an
end of all the frogs, and leave unpeopled those fair silver
lakes. It seemed that all that valiant, green, and freckled
race must perish for the sin of one alone, their coward King.
Such sorrow had he wrought by treachery and lies.

But he whom men call father Jove, who made both frogs

and mice as well as men, and shows his grace no less to frogs than to the human race, felt softest pity rising in his soul. That mice and frogs should make such worlds of slain! Alack, what gentle croakers lay there dead! Alack, what pretty nibblers would arise no more. And to what end? What purpose had been gained? No end at all, but only sorrow, tears and shame. Thus are the sorry ways of war. So Jove, in pity, hurled the lightning down to bid those warriors stay their horrid fight.

Deep lengthening thunders roll. The hills and mountains quake. But little heed the mice. Still stubborn, they advance, nor even for a thunderbolt will stay their dread design. And since the lightning cannot move those stubborn hearts, great Jove sends other aid.

From out the neighboring shore, he calls a sudden throng.

III

There comes a band of unexpected warriors pouring o'er the plain. Deformed to view, in suits of armor strong, they come with sidewise wheeling march. Their limbs have harpy claws; dread scissors guard the passage to their mouths; broad spread their shining backs; their round black eye-balls roll within their savage chests. On eight long feet and either way they go, now forward and now back, for at each end they seem to have a head. These warriors men agree to call the crabs.

Now with their harpy claws, they seize the heroes by their tails; they nip their legs; they clip their arms. Confusion falls on all, confusion wild and mad. And from that armored host, in headlong flight, run frogs and mice alike. Across the plain they flee, nor do they stop for breath till they have crept in holes and safely hid themselves from sight.

And thus came to an end the sorry struggle that arose from one unthinking act of treachery. Thus in a single day a war was fought, a whole sad Iliad in the space of one revolving sun.

The Rarest Animal of All*

HUGH LOFTING

PUSHMI-PULLYUS are now extinct. That means, there aren't any more. But long ago, when Doctor Dolittle was alive, there were some of them still left in the deepest jungles of Africa; and even then they were very, very scarce. They had no tail, but a head at each end and sharp horns on each head. They were very shy and terribly hard to catch. The black men get most of their animals by sneaking up behind them while they are not looking. But you could not do this with the pushmi-pullyu—because, no matter which way you came toward him, he was always facing you. And besides, only one-half of him slept at a time. The other head was always awake—and watching. This was why they were never caught and never seen in Zoos. Though many of the greatest huntsmen and the cleverest menagerie-keepers spent years of their lives searching through the jungles in all weathers for pushmi-pullyus, not a single one had ever been caught. Even then, years ago, he was the only animal in the world with two heads.

Well, the monkeys set out hunting for this animal through the forest. And after they had gone a good many miles, one of them found peculiar footprints near the edge of a river; and they knew that a pushmi-pullyu must be very near that spot.

*Reprinted through the courtesy of the authorized American publishers, Frederick A. Stokes Company.

Then they went along the bank of the river a little way, and they saw a place where the grass was high and thick, and they guessed that he was in there.

So they all joined hands and made a great circle round the high grass. The pushmi-pullyu heard them coming, and he tried hard to break through the ring of monkeys. But he couldn't do it. When he saw that it was no use trying to escape, he sat down and waited to see what they wanted.

They asked him if he would go with Doctor Dolittle and be put on show in the Land of the White Men.

But he shook both his heads hard and said, "Certainly not!"

They explained to him that he would not be shut up in a menagerie but would just be looked at. They told him that the Doctor was a very kind man but hadn't any money, and people would pay to see a two-headed animal, and the Doctor would get rich and could pay for the boat he had borrowed to come to Africa in.

But he answered, "No. You know how shy I am. I hate being stared at." And he almost began to cry.

Then for three days they tried to persuade him.

And at the end of the third day, he said he would come with them and see what kind of a man the Doctor was, first.

So the monkeys traveled back with the pushmi-pullyu. And, when they came to where the Doctor's little house of grass was, they knocked on the door.

Dr. Dolittle, one of the few beloved characters given children by a modern writer, grew from the letters Hugh Lofting, an English soldier in the World War, wrote his children and illustrated with his own drawings.

The duck, who was packing the trunk, said, "Come in!"

And Chee-Chee very proudly took the animal inside and showed him to the Doctor.

"What in the world is it?" asked John Dolittle gazing at the strange creature.

"Lord save us!" cried the duck. "How does it make up its mind?"

"It doesn't look to me as though it had any," said Jip, the dog.

"This, Doctor," said Chee-Chee, "is the pushmi-pullyu—the rarest animal of the African jungles, the only two-headed beast in the world! Take him home with you and your fortune's made. People will pay any money to see him."

"But I don't want any money," said the Doctor.

"Yes, you do," said Dab-Dab, the duck. "Don't you remember how we had to pinch and scrape to pay the butcher's bill in Puddleby? And how are you going to get the sailor the new boat you spoke of—unless we have the money to buy it?"

"I was going to make him one," said the Doctor.

"Oh, do be sensible!" cried Dab-Dab. "Where would you get all the wood and the nails to make one with? And besides, what are we going to live on? We shall be poorer than ever when we get back. Chee-Chee's perfectly right: take the funny-looking thing along, do!"

"Well, perhaps there is something in what you say," murmured the Doctor. "It certainly would make a nice new kind of pet. But does the er—what-do-you-call-it really want to go abroad?"

"Yes, I'll go," said the pushmi-pullyu who saw at once, from the Doctor's face, that he was a man to be trusted. "You have been so kind to the animals here—and the monkeys tell me that I am the only one who will do. But you must promise me that if I do not like it in the Land of the White Men, you will send me back."

"Why, certainly—of course, of course," said the Doctor. "Excuse me, surely you are related to the Deer Family, are you not?"

"Yes," said the pushmi-pullyu, "to the Abyssinian Gazelles and the Asiatic Chamois on my mother's side. My father's great-grandfather was the last of the Unicorns."

"Most interesting!" murmured the Doctor, and he took

a book out of the trunk which Dab-Dab was packing and began turning the pages. "Let us see if Buffon says anything . . ."

"I notice," said the duck, "that you only talk with one of your mouths. Can't the other head talk as well?"

"Oh, yes," said the pushmi-pullyu. "But I keep the other mouth for eating—mostly. In that way I can talk while I am eating without being rude. Our people have always been very polite."

When the packing was finished and everything was ready to start, the monkeys gave a grand party for the Doctor, and all the animals of the jungle came. And they had pineapples and mangoes and honey and all sorts of good things to eat and drink.

After they had all finished eating, the Doctor got up and said:

"My friends: I am not clever at speaking long words after dinner, like some men; and I have just eaten many fruits and much honey. But I wish to tell you that I am very sad at leaving your beautiful country. Because I have things to do in the Land of the White Men, I must go. After I have gone, remember never to let the flies settle on your food before you eat it; and do not sleep on the ground when the rains are coming. I—er—er—I hope you will all live happily ever after."

When the Doctor stopped speaking and sat down, all the monkeys clapped their hands a long time and said to one another, "Let it be remembered always among our people that he sat and ate with us, here, under the trees. For surely he is the Greatest of Men!"

And the Grand Gorilla, who had the strength of seven horses in his hairy arms, rolled a great rock up to the head of the table and said:

"This stone, for all time, shall mark the spot."

And even to this day, in the heart of the jungle, that stone still is there. And monkey-mothers, passing through the forest with their families, still point down from the branches and whisper to their children, "Sh! There it is! Look, where the Good White Man sat and ate food with us in the Year of the Great Sickness!"

Then, when the party was over, the Doctor and his pets started out to go back to the seashore. And all the monkeys went with him as far as the edge of their country, carrying his trunk and bags, to see him off.

"A *milkweed*, and a *buttercup*, and *cowslip*," said sweet Mary, "Are growing in my garden-plot, and this I call my *dairy*."
—Peter Newell

From *Pictures and Rhymes*, published by Harper & Brothers.

The Fisherman and His Wife

ADAPTED FROM WILHELM AND JACOB GRIMM

A FISHERMAN lived with his wife in a wretched little hovel by the sea, and every day he went out fishing. Once, as he was sitting with his rod, looking at the clear water, his line suddenly went far down below and, when he drew it out, up came a big flounder. Said the flounder, "Hark, you, fisherman, I pray you put me back in the water. I am no common fish; I am a fish who can grant people their wishes."

"Come," said the fisherman, "deliver me from a fish that talks!" With that he put the flounder back into the water, and down went the flounder to the bottom of the sea. Then the fisherman went home to his wife.

"Have you caught nothing today?" said the woman.

"I drew up a flounder," said the fisherman, "but he said he was no common fish—he was a fish who granted people their wishes, so I put him back in the water."

"Well, and what did you wish for?" asked the woman.

"Oh!" said the man, "what should I wish for? I wished for nothing. I'm quite content with what I have."

"Ah, you stupid good-for-nothing!" cried the woman. "It is surely hard to have to live always in such a wretched hovel; you might have wished for a pretty cottage. Go back and call the fish. Tell him we want a pretty cottage; he will surely give us that."

The man did not quite like to go, as he could see no reason why he should trouble the fish again. But his wife insisted, so at last he went. The water was all green and yellow now and no longer smooth as it had been before, but the fisherman stood by the sea and said:

"O Fish of the Sea, come, listen to me,
For Alice, my wife, the plague of my life,
Has sent me to beg a boon of thee."

Up came the fish. "What does she want?" he said.

"Ah!" said the man, "she says I should have asked you to grant us a wish. She does not like to live in a wretched hovel any longer. She would like a little cottage."

"Go," said the fish, "she has it already."

When the man reached home, his wife was no longer in the hovel; but, in its place, there stood a pretty cottage, and she was sitting on a bench before the door. She took him by the hand and said, "Just come inside. Isn't this better than living as we did before?"

So they went in and there was a pretty little parlor, a bedroom, and a kitchen, all fitted up with the prettiest things. Behind the house was a small yard, with hens and ducks; and a little garden, with flowers and fruit.

"Look!" said the wife. "Is not that nice?"

"Yes," said the husband, "and so we must always think it. Now we shall live quite content."

"Oh, I don't know about that!" said the wife.

Well, everything went well for a week or a fortnight, and then the woman said: "Hark you, husband, this cottage and garden are far too small for us; the fish might just as well have given us a larger house. Go to the fish and tell him to give us a great stone mansion."

"Ah, wife," said the man, "this cottage is quite good enough. Why should we live in a grand house?"

"What!" snapped the woman. "Don't you see we would be far happier in a great house than in this little cottage? Go at once!"

"No, wife," said the man, "the fish has just given us this cottage. I do not like to bother him again."

"It will be no bother to him at all," said she, "he will be glad to do it."

The man's heart grew heavy, and he said to himself, "It is not right," and yet, he went.

When he came to the sea, the water was purple and
blue and beginning to darken; he stood there and said:

"O Fish of the Sea, come, listen to me,
For Alice, my wife, the plague of my life,
Has sent me to beg a boon of thee."

Up came the fish.
"Well, what does she want now?"

"Alas," said the man, "she wants a stone mansion!"

"Go!" said the fish. "She has a mansion already."

Then the man went home and there was his wife
standing on the steps of a great stone mansion. "Come
in!" she said and she led him into a great hall, paved
with marble. Many servants flung wide the doors. In
the rooms were chairs and tables of gold, crystal chan-
deliers hung from the ceiling, and food of the very best
kind was standing on all the tables. Behind the mansion
were stables for horses with the best of carriages. There
was a magnificent park in which were stags and deer
and everything that could be desired.

"Come!" said the woman. "Isn't this beautiful?"

"Yes, indeed," said the man, "and now we will live
in this beautiful house and be content."

"Nay, husband," said the woman, "but I am already
beginning to feel that it is not large enough. We
need a palace. Go to the fish. We must have a palace!"

"Ah, wife," said the man, "why do we want a palace?
I do not want a palace."

"Well, I do!" snapped the wife. "Go to the fish!"

"But," said the man, "I do not like to ask him for anything more."

"Husband," she said, "stop talking! Go!"

So the man went. "It is not right! It is not right!" thought he, yet he went.

The sea now was quite dark gray and the waves were swelling and heaving. As he stood beside it he called:

"O Fish of the Sea, come, listen to me,
For Alice, my wife, the plague of my life,
Has sent me to beg a boon of thee."

"What does she want now?" said the fish.

"Alas!" said the man. "She wants a palace."

"Go! She is in the palace," said the fish.

So the man went and he found the mansion had become a palace. It had a great tower, a sentinel stood before the door, and soldiers were all about with kettledrums and trumpets. Inside everything was of real marble and gold, with velvet covers and great golden tassels. Then the doors of the hall were opened, and there sat his wife in all this splendor, with rings on her fingers and jewels in her hair. On either side of her stood her maids-in-waiting. He went before her and said, "It is very grand, wife; we can wish for nothing more."

"We'll see about that," said the woman. Next morning she awoke at daybreak and, from her bed, she saw the beautiful country stretching before her.

"Husband," she said, "just look out over that land. Think now! Couldn't you be king and rule over all that? Go to the fish. You must be king."

"Ah, wife," said the man, "he can't make me king. Why should I be king? I don't want to be king."

"Well," said the wife, "if you won't be king, I will!"

"Ah, wife," said the man, "I do not like to say that to the fish. Why should you want to be king?"

"Ask no more questions about it! I will be king! Go!"

So off he went. "It will not end well!" he muttered. "King! It is too shameless that she is not even yet content."

The water rose and roared. A high wind blew over the land, the clouds flew, and the leaves fell from the trees. Very sorrowfully, the man stood by the shore and called:

"O Fish of the Sea, come, listen to me,
For Alice, my wife, the plague of my life,
Has sent me to ask a boon of thee."

"What *does* she want now?" said the fish.

"Alas," said the man, "she wants to be king."

"Go home!" said the fish. "She is king."

So the man went; and, when he got home, the whole palace was made of marble; soldiers were marching before the door, blowing trumpets and beating cymbals and drums. In the house, barons, dukes, and princes were going about as servants. And when he entered, there

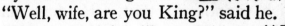

sat his wife on a golden throne; she wore on her head a golden crown set with diamonds. In one hand, she had the sceptre of gold; in the other, the orb of gold and on either side of her stood the yeomen of the guard.

"Well, wife, are you King?" said he.

"Yes," said she, "I am King!"

"And now," said the man, "do be satisfied and let well enough alone." But she looked as stiff as a post and all she said was, "I'll see about that."

Thereupon, she went to bed; but greediness let her have no sleep, for she was continually thinking what there was left for her to be that would make her greater still. At length the sun began to rise; and, when the woman saw the red of dawn, she sat up in bed and looked at it.

"Ah," she cried, "I know what there is still left for me to have. I must have power over the sun and the moon. They must only be able to rise at my command."

"Husband," said she, poking him with her elbow, "wake up! Go to the fish! I must rule over the sun and moon!"

The man was still half-asleep, but he was so startled at her words that he rolled out of bed. He thought he must have heard amiss, and rubbed his eyes and said, "Alas, wife, what are you saying?"

"Husband," she said, "if I can't order the sun and moon to rise, but have to look on and see them rise without my leave, I shall never know another happy hour."

"Alas! wife," said the man, falling on his knees before her, "the fish cannot do that. He has made you King. I beseech you do not ask that! Be content!"

Then the woman grew angry. "Go, at once!" said she. "I am King! I command you! Go!"

So the man went. But outside, a great storm was raging. It was blowing so hard, he could scarcely keep his feet. The sky was black, and the sea came in with black waves all crested with black foam. The whole earth seemed to shake, and trees came falling round about. Then the man cried, but could hardly hear his own words for the noise of the storm:

"O Fish of the Sea, come, listen to me,
For Alice, my wife, the plague of my life,
Has sent me to ask a boon of thee."

"What does she want now?" said the fish, and his voice was strange and threatening. "She wants to be Lord of the sun and the moon, so they dare not rise save at her command!"

"Go!" said the fish. "She is back in the hovel." And there they live to this very day.

How Brer Rabbit Met Brer Tar-Baby

WAY down south in the land o' cotton, when the moon hung in the sky like a great, big, round persimmon, and the mocking bird was singing in the trees, the negroes used to gather before their little cabins, to sing and play the banjo, to dance, and tell stories in the moonlight. Sometimes a little white boy or girl would slip away of an evening from the great house with the big white pillars where the owner of the plantation lived, and go down among the little pickaninnies to hear the tales and join in the fun.

All of a sudden, the banjos and the fiddles, the singing and dancing would stop, everybody would squat down in a circle, and a little old mammy with a red bandana kerchief round her head would burst out in a high, shrill laugh, her teeth shining like ivory in the moonlight. Then she would roll her eyes around to see that all the little pickaninnies were still as mice and begin to tell a story.

" 'Twa'n't my time an' 'twa'n't you' time, but 'twas a berry good time dat all de beastises got togeder—Brer Fox an' Brer Wolf an' Brer Bear an' Brer 'Possum an' all de rest, an' dey say, 'We's gwine dig a well!' All but Brer Rabbit, an' he 'low he ain't gwine wuk to dig no well. So he play roun' 'bout in de bushes an' he play roun' an' he play roun' an' he play roun'. An' de udder beastises dey say to him, 'Brer Rabbit, if you don' dig no well, wot you gwine do w'en you wants wateh?' Den Brer Rabbit he say, 'Oh, I'se gwine get it an' drink it!'

"De udder beastises dey all say, 'We's gwine plough de field an' plant co'n.' So dey all plough de field an' plant co'n. But Brer Rabbit he 'low he ain't gwine wuk to plant no co'n. So he play roun' an' he play roun' an' he play roun'. Den de udder beastises dey say to him, 'Brer Rabbit, if you don' plant no co'n, wot you gwine do w'en you wants food?' An' Brer Rabbit he say, 'Oh, I'se gwine get it an' eat it!'

"But w'en Brer Fox an' Brer Wolf an' Brer Bear an' Brer 'Possum an' all de rest, had dug de field, an' planted it, an' cut it, den Brer Rabbit he come 'long an' help hisself to de co'n. An' w'en Brer Fox an' Brer Wolf an' Brer Bear an' Brer 'Possum an' all de rest had dug de well, den Brer Rabbit he come 'long an' help hisself to de wateh.

"Den Brer Wolf an' Brer Fox an' Brer Bear an' Brer 'Possum an' all de rest, dey make up de minds to cotch Brer Rabbit, so's he cyan't drink dere wateh an' eat dere co'n no mo'! But Brer Rabbit he am too wise. He don' come to de well twice at de same time. He slip in w'en nobody ain't lookin' an' help hisself to de wateh an' de co'n, an' slip away again. So nobody cyan't cotch him.

"But Brer Wolf he say, 'By jing! I'se gwine cotch him yet!' An' he take some straw an' make it into a baby wid haid, body, ahms, laigs; an' he smear it wid tar—soft, sticky black tar, till dat dar baby's black, black as any you little pickaninnies! Den he set Tar-Baby up right dar 'side de well an' go 'way.

"Bimeby de moon come out, de whip-poor-will begin to w'istle in de swamps, an' ain't nobody awake anyw'ere at all, 'ceppin' Uncle Rastus' yaller dog a way off summ'ers howlin' at de moon. Den 'long come ole Brer Rabbit, mighty keerful-like, lookin' yere an' lookin' dere, a-listenin' fur ev'ry sound an' duckin' down behin' a stone w'en de wind go, 'Zoo-oo!' through de trees. Purty soon he come to de well an' den, wot he see in de moonshine? He see Tar-Baby settin' dar in his way, big an' black as a live pickaninny!

"Fust he gwine fur ter run, kase he thought Tar-Baby was a sure live critter; but he want to get some wateh mighty bad, so he puts on his best comp'ny mannehs an' he say, 'Good-ebenin', suh! Fine weatheh, suh!'

"But Tar-Baby ain't say nothin'.

" 'How's you' mudder, suh, an' you' grandmudder, suh, an' de chilluns, an' all de rest ob de fambly?' Brer Rabbit say, an' he creep up a leetle nearer.

"But Tar-Baby ain't say nothin'.

"Den Brer Rabbit he get mighty brave w'en he see Tar-Baby don' move, an' he drop his comp'ny mannehs an' he say, 'Look yere,' says'e, 'Get out o' my way!'

"But Tar-Baby ain't move an' ain't say nothin'.

" 'Look yere,' says Brer Rabbit again, says'e. 'You see dis yere paw,' an' he hol' up his right fo' paw, 'if you don' get out o' my way, I'se gwine hit you wid dis paw an' knock de stuffin' out o' you!'

"But Tar-Baby ain't move and ain't say nothin'! So Brer Rabbit he take his paw and blimp! he hit Tar-Baby a crack fur to knock de stuffin' out o' him, but Brer Rabbit's paw is jes' stick fast in de tar an' he cyan't pull it loose. Den Brer Rabbit begin fur to holler, 'Le' me go! Le' me go, you black rascal!' But Tar-Baby don' le' go! Den Brer Rabbit he hol' up his lef' fo' paw an' he say, 'You see dis yere paw? If you don' le' go, I'se gwine hit you wid dis paw an' knock de daylights out o' you!' But Tar-Baby don' le' go! So Brer Rabbit he take his paw an' blimp! he hit Tar-Baby anudder crack an' t'udder paw stick fast in de tar!

"Den Brer Rabbit begin fur to holler wuss'n ever, an' he say, 'Le' go! Le' go, you black rascal! You see dis yere foot! If you don' le' go, I'se gwine kick you wid dis foot an' knock you sky-high!'

"But Tar-Baby don' le' go! So Brer Rabbit he take his right foot an' blimp! he hit Tar-Baby anudder crack, an' his right foot stick fast in de tar. Den Brer Rabbit begin fur to holler like a screech owl, an' he lift up his left foot an' he say, 'Le' go! Le' go, you black rascal! You see dis yere foot? If you don' le' go, I'se gwine kick you wid dis foot an' sen' you sailin' up to de moon!'

"But Tar-Baby don' le' go! So Brer Rabbit he take his left foot an' blimp! he hit Tar-Baby anudder crack, an' his left foot stick fast in de tar! Den Brer Rabbit he get madder'n a hornet an' he say, 'Le' go! Le' go, you black rascal! If you don' le' go, I'se gwine butt you wid my haid an' knock you into bits!' But Tar-Baby don' le' go. So Brer Rabbit he butt Tar-Baby wid his haid an' his haid stick tight in de tar.

131

"Den Brer Rabbit he holler an' he screech an' he howl! But he cyan't get loose, an' dar he have to stay till de mawnin'. 'Bout sun-up 'long come Brer Wolf fur to see wot's happen, an' dar he see Brer Rabbit stuck to Tar-Baby tighter'n a burr. Den Brer Wolf he open his mouf an' laugh an' show all his toofs, an' he say, sweet as honey, 'Good-mawnin', Brer Rabbit. How is you dis fine mawnin'?'

"Now Brer Rabbit ain't say nothin', but he begin to shake in de knees, kase he know wot's comin' to 'im. An' Brer Wolf he say, 'Wot for you don' speak to me, Brer Rabbit? 'Pears like you is a little *stuck up* dis mawnin'!' An' he laugh fit to split, 'Hi, yi, yi, yi! I hear you is lookin' fur a drop o' wateh, so I'se jes' gwine take you an' frow you in de well!' An' he cotch hol' o' Brer Rabbit by de hind laig. Now Brer Rabbit he's got de shakes all ober! 'Pears like he's gwine ter en' up in de well. But he been a thinkin' an' he know he cayn't get out o' dis yere fix widout he use his wits. So he say, 'O Brer Wolf, please do frow me into de well! Dat'll gi'e me de bes' drink ob wateh I'se ebber had. Dat's jes' w'ere I wants to be—in de well. But, whatebber you do, don', don', don', please don' frow me in de brier-patch!'

"Now Brer Wolf he's mighty s'prised w'en he hear Brer Rabbit say he wants to get frowed in de well, an' so he say, 'Well den, I jes' ain't gwine frow you in de well. I'se gwine build a fire fer ter roast some o' dat co'n you'se a hankerin' atter, an' I'se gwine frow you in de fire!'

" 'O Brer Wolf! Brer Wolf!' says Brer Rabbit (but

he's shakin' like a leaf w'en he say it). 'Please do frow me in de fire. Den I'll eat all dat co'n I'se hankerin' atter. In de fire's jes' w'ere I wants to be. But, whatebber you do, don', don', don', please don' frow me in de brier-patch!'

"Den Brer Wolf he scratch his haid an' he say, 'You wants me to frow you in de well, you wants me to frow you in de fire; well den, you rascal dat plays roun', an' plays roun', an' plays roun', an' don' do no wuk, an' eats co'n udder folkeses plants, an' takes wateh out a well udder folkeses digged, I'se gwine do de wustest thing you don' want me to,—*I'se gwine frow you straight in de brier-patch!*'

"An' he yank Brer Rabbit loose from Tar-Baby an' frow him straight into de brier-patch. 'Dar now,' he say, 'de briers 'll scratch 'im, an' poke 'im, an' jab 'im! I done finish Brer Rabbit!'

"But jes' den he hear Brer Rabbit laughin' an' see him goin' lippity clippity through de briers, an' Brer Rabbit call out, 'Thank you, Brer Wolf, kind Brer Wolf! Thank you fur sendin' me straight back home! I an' all my fambly was bo'n an' raised in de brier-patch. Hi, yi, yi, yi!'"

Master of All Masters
JOSEPH JACOBS

A GIRL once went to the fair to hire herself for a servant. At last a funny-looking old gentleman engaged her, and took her home to his house. When she got there, he told her that he had something to teach her; for that, in his house, he had his own names for things.

He said to her: "What will you call me?"

"Master or mister, or whatever you please, sir," said she.

He said: "You must call me 'master of all masters.' And what would you call this?" pointing to his bed.

"Bed or couch, or whatever you please, sir."

"No, that's my 'barnacle.' And what do you call these?" said he, pointing to his pantaloons.

"Breeches or trousers, or whatever you please, sir."

"You must call them 'squibs and crackers.'

And what would you call her?" pointing to the cat.

"Cat or kit, or whatever you please, sir."

"You must call her 'white-faced simminy.' And this now," showing the fire, "what would you call this?"

"Fire or flame or whatever you please, sir."

"You must call it 'hot cockalorum,' and what this?" he went on, pointing to the water.

"Water or wet, or whatever you please, sir."

"No, 'pondalorum' is its name. And what do you call all this?" asked he, as he pointed to the house.

"House or cottage, or whatever you please, sir."

"You must call it 'high-topper mountain.'"

That very night the servant woke her master up in a fright and said, "Master of all masters, get out of your barnacle and put on your squibs and crackers. For white-faced simminy has got a spark of hot cockalorum on its tail; and, unless you get some pondalorum, high-topper mountain will be all on hot cockalorum!"

...That's all.

A TRAGIC STORY

There lived a sage in days of yore,
And he a handsome pigtail wore;
But wondered much, and sorrowed more,
Because it hung behind him.

He mused upon the curious case,
And swore he'd change the pigtail's place,
And have it hanging at his face,
Not dangling there behind him.

Says he, "The mystery I've found—
I'll turn me round,"—he turned him round;
But still it hung behind him.

Then round and round, and out and in,
All day the puzzled sage did spin;
In vain—it mattered not a pin,
The pigtail hung behind him.

And right, and left, and round about,
And up, and down, and in, and out
He turned; but still the pigtail stout
Hung steadily behind him.

And though his efforts never slack,
And though he twist, and twirl, and tack,
Alas! still faithful to his back,
The pigtail hangs behind him.

—*Albert von Chamisso.*

TRANSLATED BY WILLIAM MAKEPEACE THACKERAY

The Girl Who Used Her Wits
A CHINESE FOLK TALE

THERE lived once a long time ago in China, a woman named Fow-Chow who had two sons. These sons married young girls from a village some distance away, and when the wedding festivities were over, they brought their wives home to live with their mother.

Now Lotus-blossom and Moon-flower, the two daughters-in-law, were good and obedient young women. They were always very respectful to their mother-in-law. They waited upon her, made her tea whenever she wished it and served her her bowl of rice and stewed meat, or salt fish and vegetables, three times a day on her little carved red-lacquer table in the best blue china dishes. But, though they were always thus obedient to the head of the family, they were forever coming to the place where she sat in state in the house, bowing low before her and begging respectfully:

"Honored lady, we pray you, let us go for a few days and pay a visit in the village where we were born."

The mother-in-law grew wearied at last with their always wanting to leave home and go a-merrymaking, so she thought to herself, "I will find a way to end this once and for all."

The next time they came, bowed low before her, and made their request, she said:

"Yes, little pheasants, you may go and pay the visit in your old village. Go as soon as you like

137

But remember this—you must bring me back when you come, the only two things for which I have a desire in all the world, or you shall never again return to your husbands and your home!"

"Oh, we will gladly bring you whatever you like, honored lady!" cried the thoughtless young women.

"Very well then," said the mother-in-law, "you, Lotus-blossom, shall bring me back some fire, wrapped in a paper; and you, Moon-flower, shall bring me wind in a paper!"

So anxious were the young girls to be off, that they promised at once to bring back what the honored lady asked, without once stopping to think how they should ever be able to get such remarkable presents.

They took leave of their husbands and started at once, chatting gaily together on the way. Through the crowds of pigs and fowls and children in the village street, they tripped past rows of little one-story houses with quaintly carved, gay-colored porches, then out of the gate of the village. They had made their way well along the highway and put many a field of indigo, rice, and sugar-cane behind them, when, all of a sudden, it came over Lotus-blossom just what her mother-in-law had asked of her. She must bring back some fire wrapped in a paper or she could never again return to her husband and her home.

On the instant, Lotus-blossom stopped short in the road and began to cry. And, when Lotus-blossom began

to cry, Moon-flower stopped too and remembered what she had been ordered to bring back—wind in a paper! Who could ever do such a thing?

So Lotus-blossom and Moon-flower both flung themselves down by the roadside and cried together. "Never, never, never," they sobbed, "can we go home again."

As they sat there, along toward them from the fields came a young girl riding on a water buffalo. She stopped before them and asked, "Why are you crying?"

The only answer was, "Boo-hoo! Boo-hoo! Boo-hoo!"

"Crying will not help matters," said the girl. "It is better to consider and see if you cannot find a way out of your difficulties. Tell me what troubles you."

So at last the young women dried their tears long enough to tell her their trouble.

"Well," said the girl, "it is true you have been

thoughtless and heedless, but come home with me. We will put our heads together and see if we cannot think how to fulfill your mother-in-law's commands."

Now Lotus-blossom and Moon-flower had never even dreamed of thinking, but seeing that the girl honestly hoped to help them, they got up behind her on the water buffalo and went off with her. When they reached her father's house, they all sat down on the floor of the porch and began to consider a way out. Soon the girl sprang to her feet and ran into the house.

In a few moments, she returned; and, in her hand, she held, lo! a paper lantern as round as the moon and inside the lantern was a lighted candle!

"Ah," cried Lotus-blossom raising her hands joyously toward the lantern, "there you have it! The very thing for me to take back to my honored mother-in-law—fire wrapped in a paper!"

But Moon-flower was still frowning; she had thought of no way to fulfill her mother-in-law's command.

Their hostess thought a while longer. Then she went into the house and returned with a paper fan.

"Take this and wave it back and forth!" she cried to Moon-flower. The young wife did as she was told, and behold! the paper carried wind against her face!

"Wind in a paper!" cried Moon-flower in astonishment. "Now I, too, may return to my home!"

So the two young women gratefully took leave of the girl who used her wits. They paid the visit to their

native village and, when they had stayed long enough, they set out once more for home.

Their mother-in-law saw them coming and was greatly surprised. She did not even wait for them to come to her, but went to meet them at the door.

"Have there come to this family daughters-in-law who do not obey their mother-in-law?" she cried sternly. "Have you come here without fire wrapped in a paper and wind in a paper?"

As she spoke, Lotus-blossom held up her paper lantern with fire inside it, and Moon-flower began to send the wind against her mother-in-law's face by gently waving her paper fan.

"Well, someone has done some thinking!" the honored lady cried. "Come into the house and serve tea!" As they all sipped their tea from the dishes on the red-lacquer table, the lantern swung gaily above them and they cooled themselves with the fan.

HALLOWE'EN

Olive Beaupré Miller

IT'S nice to be little teeny, tiny bit scared
  When Hallowe'en time comes round,
And to feel the shiver-shivers and the creepy-creep-creeps
And your heart going pound, pound, pound.

Oh, a-walking up the street in the dark, dark, dark,
There's a jack-o-lantern grinning like an imp.
There's an ugly old witch with an ugly false face
Hobbling off on a cane—limp, limp!

Oh, we're awful, awful scared till we hear a little giggle
And the witch turns out to be Grace—
What next? Look out! That bony, bony arm—
There's a skeleton a-dangling in your face!

In the black, black shade, there's a white, white thing—
It's a ghost! Look, it's starting in to chase.
Run, run! That white thing's after us!
Oh, it's Tom in a sheet and pillow-case!

Teeny-Tiny

AN ENGLISH FOLK TALE

ONCE upon a time there was a teeny-tiny woman who lived in a teeny-tiny house in a teeny-tiny village.

Now, one day, this teeny-tiny woman put on her teeny-tiny bonnet, and went out of her teeny-tiny house to take a teeny-tiny walk. And when this teeny-tiny woman had gone a teeny-tiny way, she came to a teeny-tiny gate; so the teeny-tiny woman opened the teeny-tiny gate, and went into a teeny-tiny garden.

And when this teeny-tiny woman had got into the teeny-tiny garden, she saw a teeny-tiny scarecrow, and the teeny-tiny scarecrow wore a teeny-tiny bonnet and a teeny-tiny dress. And the teeny-tiny woman said: "That teeny-tiny bonnet and that teeny-tiny dress will fit my teeny-tiny self."

So the teeny-tiny woman hung the teeny-tiny dress and the teeny-tiny bonnet over her teeny-tiny arm, and then she went home to her teeny-tiny house.

Now when the teeny-tiny woman got home to her teeny-tiny house, she was a teeny-tiny bit tired; so she went up her teeny-tiny stairs to her teeny-tiny bed, and put the teeny-tiny dress and the teeny-tiny bonnet into a teeny-tiny closet. And when this teeny-tiny woman

143

had been asleep a teeny-tiny time, she was awakened by a teeny-tiny voice from the teeny-tiny closet, which said:

"Give me my clothes!"

At this the teeny-tiny woman was a teeny-tiny bit scared; so she hid her teeny-tiny head under the teeny-tiny bedclothes and went to sleep again. And when she had been asleep again a teeny-tiny time, the teeny-tiny voice cried out from the teeny-tiny closet a teeny-tiny bit louder:

"Give me my clothes!"

This made the teeny-tiny woman a teeny-tiny bit more scared; so she hid her teeny-tiny head a teeny-tiny bit further under the teeny-tiny bedclothes. And when the teeny-tiny woman had been asleep again a teeny-tiny time, the teeny-tiny voice from the teeny-tiny cupboard said again a teeny-tiny bit louder:

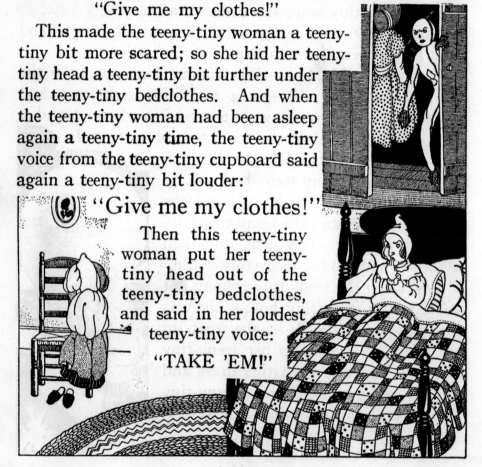

"Give me my clothes!"

Then this teeny-tiny woman put her teeny-tiny head out of the teeny-tiny bedclothes, and said in her loudest teeny-tiny voice:

"TAKE 'EM!"

Tippity Witchit's Hallowe'en

Olive Beaupré Miller

TWO round, yellow eyes glowed like little lanterns in the darkness of the barn. Those eyes belonged to a kitten by the name of Tippity Witchit. He was all jet black except for a tiny white spot on the very tip of his tail and he lay curled up in the straw with his mother, a nice yellow Tabby, and all his brothers and sisters. His eyes were still wide open while all the rest were asleep, because he was very angry. "I want to leave you, Mother, to go out and see the world." That's what he had said that day.

But his mother had said: "My darling, you are still a very small kitten. When you have grown somewhat older, you shall go out and see the world."

Tippity Witchit sulked. The idea of telling him he was only a little kitten! Giving himself a shake, he got up from the straw. He was as big as the next cat and able to meet all adventures that might befall the cat tribe—anywhere in the world! Sneaking off to the door, he slipped across the barnyard and out on the long stretch of highway that ran to the wide, wide world. Oh, what a moon was shining! It turned all the fields to silver. And little mists were rising shimmering over the meadows. He was out in a white world of moonlight with little black shadows dancing here and there on the edges. He was out like a great big cat in the mystery of the night!

The Witch, by Peter Tchaikovsky, suggests all the eerie feeling of Hallowe'en.

Strutting along on his way, shivering a little with cold, for the time was late October, he saw a field where the cornstalks stood piled up in stacks like tepees of the Indians with yellow pumpkins lying all around them on the ground. The whole field swam in moonlight. It glittered and it glistened! Tippity Witchit leapt! He bounced on down the road half-bursting with delight.

But then he saw something different. He passed a dried up garden and there stood a wild-looking scarecrow, wearing an old felt hat and an old black suit of man's clothes. That scarecrow certainly gave young Tippity Witchit a start! He quieted down in an instant. But he said to himself very boldly: "I'm a big cat, I am! I'm not afraid of a thing in all the whole, wide world!" Just the same, he trembled when

146

he came to the very next cornfield. The corn here had not been cut; it stood in ghostly rows, like a band of withered old witches. Its long dried leaves hung down like ghostly withered old arms, its tassels streamed out every which way like straggly hair on a hag. "I'm not afraid of a thing," he had to repeat to himself.

But as Tippity Witchit was looking, he thought he heard a low chuckle. A little light appeared, dancing over a meadow. Here, there, and nowhere, it went!

"Hey, there, Will-o'-the-Wisp!" he certainly heard a chorus of shrill little bell-like voices call to that impish light. And the silver mists on the fields all of a sudden seemed to have millions of bright little eyes. There were sprites there laughing in the moonlight! Their filmy, long, white robes went trailing, curling, swirling.

The minuet, *Will-o'-the-Wisps*, by the French composer, Hector Berlioz (1803-1869), shows the tiny will-o'-the-wisps dancing and flashing their specks of light through the darkness of the night

147

And the mischievous little light that was the Will-o'-the-Wisp, began to dance with the mist sprites. Hide and seek, they played till all the world seemed alive and full of strange little chuckles. Tippity Witchit chuckled and began to dance himself.

Then Tippity Witchit heard above those chuckles a cackling, a queer kind of cackling laughter like the cackles of old Biddy Hen. And, up there against the face of the big round silver moon, he saw a black figure sailing—an old lady with a tall peaked hat and a black robe floating behind her, riding along on a broomstick and stroking a huge, black cat. She sailed right across the sky; and behind her—there came in perfect triangular formation—a bevy of big, black bats soaring on big, black wings.

The Old Witch came circling and circling, lower and lower and lower, till she landed right in the field before that hag-like row of shriveled old corn witches. And, the squadron of big black bats, breaking their orderly ranks, flew and fluttered about in a dusky cloud overhead.

"Land of living kittens!" Tippity Witchit cried, "Life is exciting at last!"

THROUGH THE GATE

Cackling and cackling and cackling, the Old Witch waved her broomstick and that row of old corn witches suddenly came to life. They began to rustle a little and then to crackle and snap! They waved their long, withered arms and danced in their even rows in a kind of drill like soldiers. Their arms moved back and forth; they swayed on their long, thin bodies; their hair streamed out in the wind; and they rustled and crackled and snapped.

"Miaow, miaow, miaow!" went the old Witch's big black cat. Then hundreds of other black cats came running out of the shadows. They all began to dance, miaowing and caterwauling and making a hideous din.

"Here's something to brag about!" Tippity Witchit cried. "Won't I tell a good story when I get home again!"

But, just at that moment, Old Mother Witch looked down in the moonlight and spied young Tippity Witchit.

"Cack, cack, cack!" she laughed. "You're a nice young Thomas Cat, and the proper color for me! I've only to wave my broomstick and make you my cat forever like all these other black cats. Then you can follow me out in the wide, wide world and frolic and dance in the moonlight till the very last end of time."

The *Dance of the Goblins* by the Italian, Antonio Bazzini, gives a musical description of goblins wildly dancing.

Well, Tippity Witchit went cold and yet he was all on fire! He tingled and trembled and shivered. He wanted to join that mad throng.

"Ah, but!" said Old Mother Witch. "I see a white spot on your tail. You can never be my cat until you are, tip to nose, as black as the sky at midnight!"

Tippity crumpled up. To lose such fun for a white spot!

"Never mind, young cat. I'll remedy that spot." Old Mother Witch waved her broomstick; and, in a second of time, who came shambling along up the road, but the scarecrow out of the garden with a few little carrots and turnips gamboling along at his heels. He was swinging his long, empty sleeves and shuffling his great big feet! The limp, black legs of his pants were bending at very odd places! His black hat was jammed so far down it sat on top of his shoulders! Wild little wisps of straw-stuffing stuck out in crazy fashion! And one of his handless arms held an old watering-pot.

"Get me some ink from the shadows." Old Mother Witch called out, and the scarecrow gave one great dive into the deepest shadow. Tippity Witchit could see the blackness of night like black water pour in a smooth black stream, as out of some unseen faucet, into the watering-pot.

"Sprinkle it now on the white spot on the tail of this Thomas Cat," Old Mother Witch commanded. The scarecrow had lifted the pot and was just on the very point of pouring the ink on the white spot when, all at once, Tippity Witchit heard a miaowing and running. Something came leaping and bounding, hurrying up the road. Jerking around in surprise, Tippity Witchit saw his mother come running toward him. The ink, pouring out as he turned, missed the spot on his tail and smeared in a big black shadow out on the ground beside him.

"Tippity Witchit, don't!" his mother screeched in terror. "Keep that white spot on your tail. It's Hallowe'en, my child! If the Old Witch gets you tonight, you'll never come home again." Before she could say any more the Old Witch raised her broomstick. She flourished it in the air, and Tippity Witchit's mother was suddenly turned to china. A fine, yellow china cat shining there in the moonlight, she stood—unable to move, unable to speak a word—frozen in the very act of leaping along the road. She looked like a beautiful ornament for somebody's mantlepiece.

"Miaow! Aow! Aow!" Tippity Witchit's heart was smitten for a moment! His mother! His poor mother! But the dance was so very enticing! He wanted to caper and leap, to dance with that crazy crowd.

"Pour it on now," said the Witch.

Tippity Witchit felt creepy. His mother! His poor mother! He wished and yet he feared. Well, he was a grown-up cat! "I don't rush into things!" he threw out his chest a little. "I'll just think the matter over!"

"Cack, cack, cack," laughed the Witch. "Then come along with me, and see what you shall see and think what you shall think." She took him up on her broomstick and oh, what a thrill was that! They soared up into the air and off to a neighboring cornfield. Breathless, Tippity Witchit clutched with all four feet the handle of that old broomstick. Such a ride as that he had never had in his life!

THROUGH THE GATE

They circled over the field and Tippity saw below the corn stacked up in piles with pumpkins lying about as big and round as the moon. And the crazy cats and the scarecrows and the little carrots and turnips came gamboling through the cornstalks. Down dived the witch with a zip, alighting on the ground. Pumpkins lay all around. She flourished her magic broomstick and all at once those pumpkins suddenly started to grin. They had eyes! They had mouths! They had noses! They had little lights shining in them! Turned into jack-o-lanterns, they started to gambol, too; and the lights in their little heads went glimmering here and there, roguishly winking and blinking.

153

"Hey there, merry fellows," Tippity Witchit managed to get enough courage to shout.

Again the Old Witch raised her broomstick and this time the stacks of corn turned into Indian tepees. Before each tepee, there sat a ghostly old Indian brave. Made of thin air were those braves! They had no more real body than the filmiest kind of night clouds. Serious, grave, and stately, they sat and they smoked and they smoked! And the smoke from their long Indian pipes rolled out and lost itself in the white mist over the cornfields. They sat and they smoked and they smoked and they watched the mad dance going on.

The will-o'-the-wisps came flickering. They drew up their flames long and lean. They leapt up into the air. Whisk! They were gone altogether! The eyes of the mist sprites glittered. They trailed their white skirts and they gamboled. The jack-o-lanterns frolicked, grinning and winking their lights. The little carrots and turnips broke away from the scarecrow and tumbled with headlong somersaults into the merry-making. A thousand little, dried leaves blew in like crazy things—zipping and flipping and fluttering. The corn witches swayed themselves forward as far as they could reach on their long, thin, shriveled bodies. Old Mother Witch left her broomstick and whirled around with the scarecrow! The cats danced in crazy couples; the bats sailed, dipped, and fluttered in wild antics overhead. All the world seemed to twitter, to chuckle and cackle and snap. And above that whole merry scene, the old Moon laughed till he cried, his tears coming down to the earth in a shower of silver moonbeams.

155

"This is the life for a cat!" Tippity Witchit miaowed.
Would he pay too big a price if he gave himself up forever
to follow Old Mother Witch? What dancing! Oh, what
dancing! A hundred times, he was tempted. He followed
now here, now there, the revel of those crazy madcaps. A
hundred times, as he watched, the scarecrow dashed from
the dancing at Old Mother Witch's command to chase
after Tippity Witchit and sprinkle the ink on his tail.

But there was, by chance, one thing that Old Mother
Witch had forgotten when she turned Mother Cat into
china. She had frozen the pleading and begging in
Mother Cat's pleading eyes into a fixed expression.
So, wherever Tippity Witchit went in that wild night's
wild wanderings, his mother's eyes shone on him, begging,
pleading, imploring. That look kept just one little, small
grain of sense alive in the head of the giddy cat child.
Mother Cat couldn't talk, but still she could speak with
her eyes. And so, every time the scarecrow stole up on
Tippity Witchit, Tippity Witchit whisked off and out of
the scarecrow's reach.

For hours and hours and hours, the dance went on in
the moonlight. And then the Old Witch got impatient.
The more that little black cat kept himself out of her
clutches, the more determined she grew that she would
get him for keeps. And so, at last, she cackled to a sleek
little black girl kitten: "Go and ask that standoffish
young Thomas Cat to dance!" And the sleek, little, black
girl kitten came and miaowed very sweetly:

THROUGH THE GATE

"O won't you dance with me?"

Well, Tippity Witchit just couldn't say "no" to an offer like that. He gave up resisting completely and went waltzing off with the girl cat, out in the midst of the frolic. He whirled and he whirled and he whirled, until he was dizzy with whirling. Life was a merry-go-round, a jolly old whirligig! At last he fell down on the ground, his thoughts all whirling inside him. And now he was far out of reach of his mother's imploring eyes. The last grain of sense he had disappeared in a buzzing and whizzing. The little girl cat gave a giggle and made a sign to the scarecrow. The scarecrow came up with his inkpot; Old Mother Witch stood cackling, ready to raise her broomstick, and Tippity Witchit's last hour as a nice, homey, family cat with the love of his mother to cheer him, seemed, alas, to have struck. But just at that moment, "Oh! Ah! Ah! Oh!" a shriek burst from Old Mother Witch. The sky in the East showed pink, and the moon dipped suddenly down over the edge of the world. Dawn, the dawn was coming! The sun sent a warning beam!

In an instant that mad world changed. Tippity Witchit came to and opened one eye to see it.

The leaves flopped down and lay still, so did the carrots and turnips. The will-o'-the-wisps and mist sprites disappeared as by magic! The bats flew off in

157

a twinkling! The old Indian braves at their smoking vanished into thin air, their tepees were stacks of corn; the jack-o-lanterns were pumpkins! The scarecrow flew back to his garden to be nothing more than a scarecrow! The ghostly old corn witches were only rows of dried corn. And Old Mother Witch, what a change! She turned into a spider—hurrying, hurrying, hurrying to roof herself over with cobwebs and hide close down to the earth. The black cats turned into ants and scurried away at a great rate. And that was the end, for a year, of that madcap Hallowe'en revel! Only one night a year to gambol in the moonlight. All the rest of time to be nothing more than an ant! Tippity Witchit shivered! What he had escaped!

"Miaow! Miaow!" he began to call for his mother. And, at that moment, flash! A sunbeam struck Mother Cat. In one brilliant sparkle of light, Mother Cat was released from the spell that bound her in china. She sprang up high in the air. Then she leapt up to Tippity Witchit and took him by his ear. "Now, we'll go home," she said, "and don't you go wandering again until you are really as big as you thought yourself tonight!"

And Tippity Witchit said, "Miaow!" But what he meant by that, you will have to guess for yourself.

The Blacksmith*
A STORY OF THE SONG BY JOHANNES BRAHMS

ONCE there was a mighty blacksmith. He had a great forge in the village where men came, bringing their horses when the horses needed new shoes. The smith held the horse's hoof firmly between his knees while he took the nails out of the horseshoe and he did the work swiftly but gently so he never hurt the horse.

Then he took down from the wall, different sizes of horseshoes. He tried these on the horse till he had one that nearly fitted. Now, with his long black tongs, he put the shoe in the fire. Wheeze! How he blew his big bellows! The flames leapt high in the air and up the big black chimney. He heated the shoe red hot. Still glowing red from

*In *The Smith*, music for a poem by Uhland, Johannes Brahms (1833-1897) tells the story of the blacksmith and gives a vivid picture of the bright sparks flying from the anvil.

the flames, he carried it to his big anvil. Taking his mighty hammer, he lifted his strong right arm and ring, ding, sing, ring, ding! How he hit that horseshoe! Ring, ding, sing, ring, ding! Sparks flew up from the anvil, a shower of golden sparks going flick, fleck off in the air.

And when he had shaped the shoe just to fit the horse's hoof, he dipped it in a pail of water. Siss! How it hissed as it cooled! Then the blacksmith nailed the shoe on the horse's hoof again, and off went the horse well shod so he would not stumble and fall or hurt his feet on rough ground.

Well, people came to watch the blacksmith from every part of the village. It was something to see the mighty, rhythmic sweep of the big smith's arm in the glow of the light from the fire as he struck the red-hot horseshoe. It was something to hear the music of his hammer on the anvil, and to watch the fierce little sparks flick angrily up in the air. Often the pretty lassie who was to marry the blacksmith would come and watch him, too.

"His face is dirty," some people said. "It's black with soot from his forge."

But the pretty lassie answered: "I love to see my sweetheart swinging his mighty hammer! I love to hear his anvil ringing! It rings out on the air like the chiming of silver bells. Big and strong, he stands in the smoke of the great black chimney. I love the roar of his bellows. I love the blaze of the flames and the sparks that fly up around him!" And she looked at the blacksmith proudly and he smiled back at her.

"The Anvil Chorus" from the opera, *Il Trovatore*, by Verdi, is sung by the blacksmiths, as they strike their hammers on their anvils, and reproduces all the music of that sound.

The Story of Big Paul Bunyan*
A TALE OF AMERICAN LUMBER CAMPS

PAUL BUNYAN was a great big man. My, but he was a giant! Why, even when he was a baby, Paul Bunyan was so enormous his mother had to put him in a lumber wagon instead of a baby carriage and she couldn't find any buttons big enough to fasten his clothes until some men in the neighborhood gave her the wheels off their wheelbarrows to sew on his baby jacket!

Paul went to live in a cave way up north in Canada. He lived all alone by himself except for his big dog Niagara. Niagara used to go out and bring back meat from the moose herds that wandered around through the forests. Well, one day when Niagara had gone away on a hunt, it began to snow from the north. That was a snow, I tell you! It fell down blue from the skies. Blue snow and blue snow and blue snow until all the frozen lakes, the rivers, hills and valleys, and the great big, tall pine trees were covered with a blue blanket as sparkling blue as the sky.

*Tales of Paul Bunyan, mighty hero of American lumberjacks, are told around their campfires. French-Canadians, Scandinavians, Irish, all the races forming the melting-pot of these camps, have added touches to this tale.

It was very pretty to see, but Paul began to wonder what had become of Niagara, for the dog had gone out to hunt before the snow began and he did not come home again. All the bighorned moose and the clumsy, big black bears had run away from the snow and Niagara had chased them as far as the North Pole.

So Niagara did not come back and Paul put on his snowshoes and his great, big mackinaw coat of blue-and-orange checks and he started out to look for him. For five whole days he looked, but he didn't see a living creature and he didn't hear a single sound in the great big lonesome blue forests, only now and then in the stillness, the frost going crackle, crackle, snap! So Paul went back to his cave feeling very sad and lonely and he laid himself down to sleep beside the fire in his cave.

THROUGH THE GATE

All of sudden—boom! Boom, boom! Boom, boom! Crash! Bang! What a noise he heard! It came from the ocean near his cave. Jumping up, Paul looked out. There lay the shining blue world glittering and swimming in moonlight, and out of the ocean was rising a great enormous white wave that rolled up on the blue sands. Paul pulled on his boots and hurried down to the water.

Ice cakes were floating about; but sticking up above them, Paul suddenly saw two ears—two enormous pointed ears. Wading out in the water, he seized hold of the ears. He tugged and he tugged and he tugged and he lifted up first a head, then a pair of shoulders and forelegs, then a body and a pair of hips, then rear legs and a tail. A calf—that's what he held—a long-legged spindling calf half-dead from being in the water, but wondrously showing in the moonlight to be as blue as the snow! Well, that was a shock to Paul! But if there could be blue snow, there could surely be a blue calf.

The blue calf scarcely breathed as Paul took it back to the cave; he laid it by the fire and worked over it all night.

By and by in the morning the calf opened one of its eyes, suddenly stuck out its tongue, and licked Paul in the neck. Tickle, tickle, tickle went the tongue; and Paul started in to laugh. He laughed till he roared like thunder and set all the cave to rocking. And he said to himself it was well he had found this blue calf, Babe, to take the place of Niagara and keep him company in his cave. The father and mother of the calf had run away, it seemed, in fear of the strange blue snow, and their helpless child had fallen from a high cliff into the water.

Paul made some moose-moss soup in a great big black iron kettle and took it to Babe to drink. Babe drank the soup in three gulps, then he looked up playfully with a rougish twinkle in his eye, and took a huge bite of the kettle! Swishing his tail with joy, he chewed the kettle down, too. That made Paul laugh again and while he was all doubled up, roaring with thunderous laughter, the calf leapt up and butted him with terrific force from behind. Paul flew up, hit the ceiling, and came down kerplunk on the floor; but now he laughed more than ever.

"There's strength in that calf," he said. And when he saw how Babe could bellow and paw and snort like an ox ten times his age, Paul began to think to himself: "Such a great store of power ought not to go to waste. It ought to be harnessed up and put to some useful work."

And that night he had a dream. Paul saw in his dream a forest full of great big trees. And there came through the forest, a flame of fire shaped like the blade of a scythe. It cut through all the trees and they fell crash bang to the ground. And Paul woke up and said: "That's the work for Babe and me, to cut down big trees in the forests that they may be sawed into wood and made into homes for men."

So one fine day he set out with Babe behind him frolicking and bellowing very gaily. They galloped over hills and valleys, leaving Canada behind and crossed over into Michigan, looking for work, work, work. By and by they came to a forest, a great enormous huge forest of great enormous huge trees that seemed to reach up and up, and up and up to the skies. Paul cut down the trees and Babe dragged whole forests to the river to float them to the mills where they could be sawed into lumber.

In time other loggers came wishing to work for Paul till he had a great big camp of great big mighty men. There were Beeg Anatole, Mark Beaucoup, and Joe Muffraw—French Canadians. There was Angus MacIlroy, the Scotchman; and Tinty Hoolan, the Irishman. But the only one of these men who could manage Babe, the blue ox, was a big Swede named Hels Helsen, the roaring Bull of the Woods.

Every single morning, Babe was so eager to get to work that he galloped off madly to the forest with Hels holding on to his halter. Babe jerked Hels off his feet, hurled him into the air, bounced him over rocks and stumps and dragged him along on the ground; while Hels kept yelling "Har noo!" as he tried to quiet him down.

Well, these men all lived in the woods. In the daytime they cut trees which Babe hauled down to the river. At night they told stories in the open under the shining stars and then they went to bed in bunks in the big bunkhouses. When Paul's men had cut all the trees in the state where they were working, they would pack up and journey away into another state. They put the cookhouse on a sledge and hitched the bunkhouses behind and Babe drew the whole line of buildings with Paul and Hels walking beside him shouting gee, haw, and yay!

166

THROUGH THE GATE

Over hill and valley, over prairie and mountains, Babe pulled that line of buildings. The loggers rode in the bunkhouses, waving gaily at strangers as they passed along on their way. Thus they journeyed over Maine and Michigan, Wisconsin, Minnesota, Illinois, the Dakotas, Kansas, Iowa, Utah, and wherever there were trees.

They set up camp wherever they were and their camp-houses were all as big as mountains. When the loggers sat down for supper at the long tables in the cookhouse, the waiters, carrying dishes, raced around on roller skates, the place was so enormous; and the Galloping Kid, the head waiter, rode up and down the huge dining-room mounted on a big horse.

The first cook Paul ever had, a man named Pea-soup Shorty, wouldn't feed the men anything except pea-soup and hardtack, so Paul hired Hot Biscuit Slim, and there was a man who could cook! Hot Biscuit Slim fed the loggers griddlecakes with maple syrup, bacon, ham and eggs, mashed potatoes and gravy, green corn and roasted duck; and he had working under him a man named Cream Puff Fatty who made delicious cream puffs, pumpkin pies, frosted cakes, jelly rolls, gingerbread, jam tarts, and sugared doughnuts as big as platters. Thanks to these marvelous cooks, life in camp was a joy.

THROUGH THE GATE

But one day a very great danger threatened
Babe, the blue ox. Paul had his own home
camp in the Smiling River Country under
Rock Candy Mountain, a very beautiful
mountain that looked like white ice-cream.
Paul had not been to this camp for seven
years at least, and it was now a farm where he got the
food for his loggers. John Shears and a lot of farmers
worked this farm for Paul, taking care of the fields and
gardens, the turkeys, ducks and geese, the chickens,
pigs and cows. John raised so much food that it took
10,000 horse-teams, driven in endless lines under Shagline
Bill, to carry it all from the farm to the loggers up in
the woods. So John grew very puffed up. John Shears,
well, he was somebody, to run a farm like that! John
began to think wickedly, that if he could manage to
wipe all the loggers out of the world, all men would have
to be farmers. And if all men were farmers,
they would make John Shears their boss
instead of the big logger, Paul.
One day he said to himself:

"By gravy, I know what
I'll do! I'll get Babe out of
the way! He hauls the logs
to the river. Without that
dad-binged blue ox there
wouldn't be nary a chance
o' carryin' on at loggin'!"

And he thought and thought and thought how he could get rid of Babe. At last he hit on a plan, a very terrible plan. Every year, it seems, John had to send up to camp Babe's favorite food of parsnips. But if he cut down in the fields the first growth of these parsnips, the second growth came up poison. Now there was an idea! He would send Babe poison parsnips! Those parsnips would certainly kill him. And what could ever be surer to put an end to logging? Well, John told his farmers his plan and they cried "Hurrah!" and joined in it. "Three cheers for the farmers!" they shouted. "We'll be the world's big men!"

But there was one man on the farm, whom the farmers thought such a mere nobody that they never said anything to him about their wicked plan. This was poor Little Meery, the slavey on the farm. He had once been Thomas O'Meery, the famous Irish Orphan, a most

ambitious young logger and he had worked for Paul out in the great big forests. But, alas, the rich food served in camp by Hot Biscuit Slim and Cream Puff Fatty had made Little Meery so fat he could no longer swing an ax. He grew so round and so fat, that, if he chanced to fall down, he could never get up again. He just had to roll around until somebody came along and set him up on his feet.

THROUGH THE GATE

One day while he still worked out in the forest-camp, he fell and rolled down hill. Bang! He bumped into some loggers and smashed them flat as pancakes so they couldn't get up for weeks. Naturally after that, Paul couldn't have him logging; so he sent him off to the farm. But John Shears despised Little Meery. He set him to washing dishes and carrying slops to the pigs. The farmers all made fun of him. When they wanted to call him they'd cry, "Here, chick! Here, chick, chick, chick!" just as they called the chickens and they made him sleep on a bunk under the kitchen sink.

But all this cruel treatment Little Meery endured with sweetness. When his day of toil was over, he would pick a bunch of pink clovers, tuck Porkums, his little pet pig, under his fat little arm, waddle across the foot bridge that ran over Honey Creek and sit down on a log to enjoy the one pleasure he had. This pleasure was to imagine that he was a tall, lean logger, able to swing his ax with such powerful and telling blows that even the great Paul Bunyan thought him a mighty hero.

171

One day Little Meery, pretending to chop down trees in a great tree-felling contest, was swinging his arms about in such a violent fashion that he fell and could not get up. He rolled down as far as the bridge; but there he got stuck fast, the bridge was so very narrow. He stayed there wedged in tight until noon of the following day. But at dinner time John Shears, coming back to the farmhouse, found the breakfast dishes unwashed. So he set out in a rage to find Little Meery and beat him. He beat him all afternoon, only stopping five minutes out of every hour to rest his arm a bit.

Well, Paul, of course, was supposed to be way up in the woods when all this was going on, but as John stood beating Little Meery, what should they see in the twilight, but Babe loping quickly along with the whole long train of camp buildings trailing along behind. Flashing with windows alight, they streaked swiftly by in the darkness like a railroad train in the night.

Leaving Babe to go on under direction of Hels up to the big farm buildings, Paul came and stood face to face with that rascally farmer, John Shears. John Shears was mighty surprised. He let Little Meery go in a hurry and said they two had only been playing a pleasant game. Paul didn't suspect the truth. He never suspected evil in his great big generous heart. He said he'd come to the farm to cut down such trees as still stood in the forests about the place. "Let Babe have plenty of *parsnips*," he ordered Babe's favorite food.

THROUGH THE GATE

But at the mention of parsnips, John Shears pricked up his ears. That would just fit in with the wicked plan he was hatching. "Parsnips, he wants me to feed him!" John cackled to himself with delight. "Dad gum if that ain't funny! Well, parsnips he'll surely git!" And he made up his mind to feed those poison parsnips to Babe the very first chance he got when Paul should be out of the way. Well, very soon Paul went off. He had to look over the trees in the district round about and he took Hels, the Big Swede, with him. There wasn't a big boss left to guard the life of poor Babe. Then John set his men digging parsnips in a perfect frenzy of hurry. For twenty-hours every day, those farmers dug parsnips and parsnips.

Meantime, the mighty loggers, left with no work to busy them till Paul should come home again, tramped over Rock Candy Mountain. They ate great handfuls of fruit off the strawberry trees and plucked hunks of maple sugar from the beautiful maple trees. In the afternoons they gamboled over the clover fields which were very pink and fragrant and they swam in the old swimming-holes along the Smiling River.

My, what meals they had with all the fresh stuff on the farm! Cream Puff Fatty made them delicious short-cake and Hot Biscuit Slim made gravy over the new potatoes out of real farm cream. He gave them so much green corn that the cobs were piled mountain-high. So the loggers were very happy and they never dreamed of the wicked plot the farmers had made against Babe. Babe enjoyed himself, too. The loggers turned a Lemonade Spring so it ran into the barn, and Babe lived high on clover with lemonade ever flowing into his drinking-trough.

Everybody on the farm was happy except poor fat Little Meery. He saw the loggers about, the great, big, mighty men, and he did so want to be one of them and share their life again. Never had the scouring of pots and the feeding of pigs seemed to him such wretched business. Had it not been for the squeals with which piggie Porkums tried to comfort him, he'd have had no one at all to give him a bit of love. One night as he lay on his bunk under the kitchen sink, crying alone by himself, he heard John Shears in the sitting-room talking to his farmers. There they all sat in rocking-chairs around the center table that held the sitting-room lamp.

"The parsnips is ready," said John. "We'll feed 'em tonight to that ox-crittur and pizin him dead as a door-nail! Then there'll be no more loggin' and farmers 'ull boss the world!" At hearing these awful words, Little Meery was so surprised that he crashed his head, bang, on the sink, making a terrible racket.

"Who's that?" One of the farmers gave a guilty start.

"Oh, it's only Little Meery," another one said with scorn.

By and by the farmers went out into the night. Little Meery got up and looked out the kitchen door. A moon rode high in the sky shining over the barnyard. Little Meery could see the farmers all lined up in rows around the barnyard fence; and, in the center of the yard, gleaming deadly white in the moonlight, was a huge pile of poison parsnips. John Shears went to the stable and opened the great stable door. Babe soon appeared in the doorway, gentle and unsuspicious. Look now, he spied the parsnips! He sniffed their pleasant smell. In a moment more he would eat them!

Poor Little Meery! Good gracious! What in the world could he do? Fright and despair seized his soul when suddenly, buzz, buzz, hum, what a noise he heard! Since the clover had been cut, two big bees, Bum and Bill, had been kept locked in the beehive and they were very angry since their honey was only half-gathered. Buzzing now in the hive, they made a roar like thunder. Little Meery had an idea. Here was one chance to save Babe. Slipping out of the door, Little Meery opened the hive! The bees shot out like bullets. They spied Babe at the parsnips! They flew in a beeline for him! They settled down on his back and began a furious stinging. Babe stopped sniffing the parsnips. He bellowed with the force of a whirlwind.

THROUGH THE GATE

The terrible snort of his breath raised such a gust of air, that it blew all the farmers sky-high. John Shears rushed out to the ox to drive the bees away; but just at that moment Babe, trying to reach Bum and Bill, lifted his hind leg to kick. Zip, he caught John with his leg! He hurled him so high in the air, John sailed over Rock Candy Mountain, and was not seen for three weeks. Pawing the earth in distress, raising up clouds of dust, swishing his great big tail, Babe bucked and he kicked and he leapt. He stood on his head and his horns, he flung himself down and rolled over. But still Bum and Bill would not budge.

At last, at last, and at last, just as Little Meery had hoped, Babe ran back to his stable rubbing the bees off his back as he scraped through the narrow doorway and banging the door behind him with his kicking, plunging, and floundering. There he was safe from the parsnips! And there were Bum and Bill still buzzing at the stable door, to keep him shut up inside.

Well, that was a good deed done! Little Meery had saved the blue ox. But where now was Little Meery? He had been blown by Babe's bellow into the very midst of the scrambling and floundering farmers. But fortunately, for him, he had landed on his feet; so he ran off toward the footbridge with the farmers all chasing after him. They were right on his heels, just grabbing him by his coat tail, to give him a good, sound beating when all at once the loggers came and fell on the farmers. They all piled up on the bridge on top of Little Meery. Then what a battle followed! All night long they fought! Jaw-hammering, hair-yanking, nose-pounding! But just the same Babe, in the stable, mooed safely in his stall while Bum and Bill buzzed outside.

With sunrise Paul came back. "What's going on here?" he thundered, and the sound of his earth-shaking voice made the farmers and loggers collapse.

Paul roared at the men to explain what had caused such a terrible battle. But the farmers and loggers were now, every one so worn out and weary that they just lay still in their heap unable to speak a word. Only Little Meery, down at the bottom of the pile with no more than his head sticking out, could find strength to raise his voice and whisper the horrible story. And when Paul Bunyan heard how Little Meery had saved his beloved blue ox, Babe, he cried: "You're a man and a hero! What can I do, my friend, to reward you in some small measure for what you did last night?"

"O take me back as a logger," Little Meery cried. "That's all I want in the world!" But Paul shook his head and said sadly: "A logger must be lean! You're too fat, Little Meery!" Then Little Meery managed to wriggle out from under the pile of wearied men.

And lo and behold! the weight of all that heavy heap had mashed all the extra fat off him. He was as lean as a logger! Paul could scarcely believe his eyes.

"By the whistling, old bald-headed jeem cris, you shall be a logger again!" Paul cried with a thunderous shout.

Thus Little Meery gained his heart's desire. He became one of the toughest, mightiest loggers in the forests and neither Hot Biscuit Slim nor Cream Puff Fatty could ever tempt him again to put on an ounce of fat.

After three-weeks' time, John Shears returned very humble from the place over Rock Candy Mountain whither Babe's kick had sent him. He said he was sorry for what he had done and ready to take any punishment Paul might order for him. He fully expected, of course, that he would be made to eat gravel or sand for a month or two at least. But the good and mighty Paul Bunyan only said, "Get back to your work!"

So Babe was saved for logging, and for years and years after that Paul Bunyan and his men cut down the forests of America to make homes for the people. And the name of big Paul Bunyan and his mighty blue ox, Babe, will be remembered in lumber camps as long as men fell trees.

179

MY BOOK HOUSE

A SONG OF THE CANADIAN LUMBERJACK

A FOLK-SONG TRANSLATED FROM THE CANADIAN FRENCH

O, all the raftsmen, where are they?
To winter camp they've gone away,—
    Bang on the rim!
Make way! Let pass the raftsmen!
Bang on the rim! Bang, bang!

In bark canoes they paddle gay,
Up Ottawa's stream they steer their way:
    Bang on the rim!
Make way! Let pass the raftsmen!
Bang on the rim! Bang, bang!

180

THROUGH THE GATE

They've put small boots on their big feet
At Ma'am Gauthier's they dance and eat,—
    Bang on the rim!
Make way! Let pass the raftsmen!
Bang on the rim! Bang, bang!

They've stopped at Bytown on the way,
To dress themselves in clothing gay,—
    Bang on the rim!
Make way! Let pass the raftsmen!
Bang on the rim! Bang, bang!

They've come to winter camp, hooray!
They've cut axe-handles straight away—
    Bang on the rim!
Make way! Let pass the raftsmen!
Bang on the rim! Bang, bang!

Amazed, the Ottawa's waters stay,
Such noise those axes make all day,—
    Bang on the rim!
Make way! Let pass the raftsmen!
Bang on the rim! Bang, bang!

When camp is over, where are they?
They've gone back home without delay—
    Bang on the rim!
Make way! Let pass the raftsmen!
Bang on the rim! Bang, bang!

They kiss their wives and sweethearts gay,
They're glad to be back home to stay,—
    Bang on the rim!
Make way! Let pass the raftsmen!
Bang on the rim! Bang, bang!

This picture was taken from an old print in the Chateau de Ramezay, Montreal.

Old Stormalong*

A YARN OF AMERICAN SAILORS

IN DAYS when the Flying Cloud was the fastest ship on the seas, old wooden sailing vessels, their white sails flying in the wind, used to sail like sea birds out of Salem, Boston, Nantucket, and New Bedford. They carried the American flag to China, India, Java, and all the ports of the world. And their sailormen used to sing:

"How do you know she's a Yankee clipper?
    Blow, boys, blow!
The Stars and Stripes, they fly above her,
    Blow, my bully boys, blow!"

Now the greatest of all Yankee sailors was Alfred Bulltop Stormalong, just called Stormy for short, a jolly old sea dog with a circle of whiskers under his chin.

*Old Stormy is the hero of Yankee deep-sea sailors. On all the seven seas, jolly tars hailing from Salem, Boston, Newburyport, or other New England ports, have told tales and sung songs of Old Stormy.

Stormy was born on the seacoast up in the State of Maine. His father was a Yankee skipper, and all his folks followed the sea. It was written in the family Bible, that one of his great-great-grandfathers helped Noah build the ark and keep it afloat through the flood; so Stormy, no fooling about it, came of seafaring people.

Stormy was strong as a whale. Even as a baby, he could swim in the water as slick as an eel in a keg of oysters.

Well, Stormy went to sea very early. He was quick to learn about ships and soon he could sail any windjammer that ever followed the trade winds out on the briny ocean.

One of Stormy's earliest voyages was on a whaling ship, the tough old Gridiron out of New Bedford. His pal on that ship was the one-legged cook, Billy Peg Leg. Billy always kept a fiddle hanging beside the griddle on which he cooked his pancakes and he played that fiddle for dances. Stormy danced the sailor's hornpipe while Billy played on his fiddle, and how Stormy shook his legs! He planted them down on the deck with such tremendous force that the very timbers of the ship shivered and shivered and shook. And he sang at the top of his voice:

"I've a pal called Bill Peg Leg
With one leg, a wood leg,
And Billy, he's a ship's cook
And lives upon the sea.
And hanging by his griddle
Old Billy keeps a fiddle
For fiddling in the dogwatch
When the moon is on the sea!"

A good thing it was for Stormy that he had a friend in the cook; for Stormy was a huge eater. He kept a whole line of men running from the cook's galley and bringing him food in wheelbarrows; and when he had whale soup, nothing short of a Cape Cod boat was big enough to serve as a soup plate. Whale steak rare and sharks' fins, with ostrich eggs, big as cocoanuts, boiled or poached, on toast—that was what Stormy ate.

When Stormy was off duty, he sat around on a barrel, whittling birds and seals, rings and tops out of wood, or carving pictures of ships on whale's teeth or walrus' tusks. You can see his scrimshaws still in museums in the East.

Well, the Gridiron was out in the ocean chasing after whales and whaling was a dangerous business; for the whale family all kept house only where the water was deepest, right in the middle of the ocean. You couldn't coax a mama or a papa whale or even a runaway baby whale, skylarking on his own account, into shallow water. So whaling vessels sailed off on trips of four or five years, into the Pacific, the Atlantic, and the Indian Ocean. They even sailed up North and got stuck in the great towering ice fields of the frozen Arctic Ocean. Old Stormy carried candy—generally saltwater taffy—not only to pretty brown maids who lived in the South Sea Islands, but also to Eskimo girls who were all wrapped up in furs till they looked like polar bears in the region around the North Pole. There wasn't a corner of the world where those whalers didn't travel to work and play.

The great whales cruised the seas until a sailor, on the mast head, spied one spouting like a fountain. Then he shouted, "Thar she blows!" Small boats were dropped from the vessel and drew up alongside the whale. A moment of hushed expectation, then: "Stand up and let him have it!" The man, who steered the nearest small boat, would carefully poise his harpoon on the end of its great long rope and fling the spear into the whale. Well, naturally, the whale didn't like that harpoon at all. He began to churn the sea with his splashing and maybe he rushed off like mad dragging the small boat after

him—a jolly little ride through the water, jokingly called by the whalers "taking a Nantucket sleigh ride." Or maybe that whale just sank; and, suddenly, came up again right under the little boat sending the small boat flying and tossing men into the sea. And, when at last the whale had given its final lurch, turned its belly up to the sun, and consented to be whale oil to light the lamps of America, the great beast had to be towed back to the sailing ship. Fastened with ropes alongside, it was cut into strips of blubber, that were hoisted aboard the vessel and boiled in pots on deck to get out the precious whale oil.

Well, that was the kind of life the ordinary whaler led; but, with Stormy, it was different. No whale in the ocean ever played any tricks on Stormy. And they never had to put small boats out from Stormy's vessel; for Stormy was so strong, he could pull the hugest whale right straight up to the big boat. No sooner did the man in the lookout spy a whale spouting ahead and yell out, "Thar she blows!" than Stormy threw his harpoon, speared the enormous creature, and dragged it up to the ship before you could say Jack Robinson. All whales were afraid of Stormy. Why, when they so much as got wind that he was coming their way, all the whale papas and mamas called their little whales to them and took them off in a flutter, leaving their homes in a hurry and even deserting their furniture!

But once, when the whaling fleet was riding the waves at anchor on the whaling grounds of the North Atlantic,

THROUGH THE GATE

Old Stormy suddenly sighted a whole big school of whales going off on a whale schoolpicnic in charge of their whale schoolteacher. The skipper gave the order at once to hoist anchor and follow those whales. But, when the sailors rushed off and tried to raise the anchor, they found they could not lift it. They pulled and hauled and tugged; it would rise up just a little, then hands seemed to clutch it and drag it back to the bottom. Once they got it up far enough to see it was a wicked looking devilfish holding the anchor down.

The mate gave a yell for the skipper and the skipper came running in a hurry. But, before he got to the rail, Stormy had leaped overboard with his knife between his teeth. He dived down and faced that monster. With some of his numerous arms, that stubborn old devilfish had fast hold of the cable that held the anchor of Stormy's vessel; and, with the rest of his arms, he was holding to the rocks and seaweed that lay along the sea floor. Bent on mischief he was, that obstinate old rascal! He was just going to hold that anchor fast to the bottom of the sea to the very last end of time.

Well, Stormy set on that devilfish and there was a terrible tussle! The devilfish loosened a few of his arms, while he still held the cable with the rest, and he twined those slimy arms round and round Old Stormy. But Stormy's strength was terrific. He wrenched himself free of the devilfish; he looked him straight in the eye and he took his knife and went after him. They fought for

189

an hour or two; but the devil-fish had to give up. He just couldn't stand against Stormy. He lay down at last and curled up. Then Stormy took the arms of that devil-fish and he tied them together in sailor's knots, so the monster could never untie them. After that, he freed the anchor and swam back to his ship, leaving the poor old devilfish trying to untie the knots.

After this great adventure, Stormy's fame spread so quickly that he was invited to sail on the great big Albatross, a four-master out of Boston, and the hugest ship on the ocean. Man alive! That vessel was huge! Boston Harbor wasn't big enough to hold her! The masts reached up to the skies and they had big hinges on top so they could be bent down to let the sun and moon go by; and even at that, now and then, they knocked a few stars out of place. A hundred sailors, relieving each other and taking turns at looking, couldn't see the top of those masts, and thirty-four men were required to turn the steering-gear. Only Stormy could do it alone. But, with Stormy at the wheel, that ship could ride any hurricane that ever blew over the ocean.

Well, Stormy traveled all over the world for years and years on his vessels. His days were one long succession of white sails and foam-flecked seas with porpoises leaping at play and flying fish skimming like butterflies from one wave to another. Many a night he drifted in the soft, warm dusk of the tropics, with lights of a city gleaming far away on the shore. Many a time he wandered in perfumed bazaars of the East or entered, with all sails flying, into ports of many ships.

So long as Old Stormy was steering and holding the wheel of a ship—that pleasant old dame, Mother Carey, who screeches in the storm clouds, could screech as loud as she wished. But, try as she would, she could never send Old Stormy's ship to the bottom. Old Stormy was too good a sailor.

But one day, alas and alack, Old Stormy died at sea. All the sailors on the ocean mourned his going and they gave him a beautiful funeral. Mermaids and sea horses followed him, swimming in one long parade led by Nep-

tune, the King of the Ocean.   And a spooky procession of
ghost ships—the ghosts of all wrecked vessels—came up from
the Land of Phantoms, led by the Flying Dutchman.* They
flitted over the water like so many thin, white spectres to
pick Old Stormy up and carry him to Fiddler's Green,
which is the sailor's heaven.   And everyone sang in his
honor, this beautiful funeral song:

"Oh, Stormy's dead and gone to rest.
    To my way, Stormalong:
Of all the sailors he was the best.
    Aye, aye, aye, Mister Stormalong!

A good old skipper to his crew.
    To my way, Stormalong!
An able sailor, brave and true.
    Aye, aye, aye, Mister Stormalong!"

*The Overture to *The Flying Dutchman*, by Richard Wagner, shows the faint, thin spectre of a ghost ship
gliding eerily through the storm with all the crash and discord, the raging fury of wind and wave.

Pecos Bill, the Cowboy*

A TALL TALE OF AMERICAN COWBOYS

PECOS BILL was a cowboy out in the wild Wild West. He lived, when he was a baby, with his mother, who was the Old Woman, and his father, who was the Old Man, and his sixteen brothers and sisters in a little log cabin in Texas. The day after Bill was born, his mother wrapped him up cozy in a great big shaggy black bearskin and she gave him his pappy's bowie knife and left him to play with himself while she went over to the fire-place to make the corn-pone for breakfast.

Bill was kicking and crowing, when Hi-yi! Ki-yi! Ow-wow! A band of fifty Indians in the best make of feather headdresses burst right in at the door! They all made a grab for the baby but the Old Woman wouldn't have that. She just grabbed up her broomstick and hit out right and left. She lit into all those Indians! She banged 'em over the head and made her broomstick fly till she laid 'em all out cold. Then she swept 'em out the door and tidied up the room again.

*Pecos Bill is the hero of the cowboys. He came from the Pecos River region, in Texas, and his skill as a cattleman was unrivalled. His mighty deeds have been told by generations of cowmen.

Well, after that, the Indians let Baby Bill alone. The Old Woman gave the baby a grizzly bear cub to play with, then she went out to the barnyard and got herself hitched up with her oldest boy to the plough. You see the Old Man was planning to plough up a field for corn, but he didn't have any horses and he didn't have any oxen. So he hitched up his Old Woman with Towhead, the oldest boy, and he walked beside the plough, holding the reins in his hand.

Well, Towhead and the Old Woman were walking up the furrow as quiet and as gentle as any farmer could wish, when all of a sudden, zip! Up flew a piece of white paper, dancing and whirling and flipping. The Old Lady spied that paper! She gave a big jump and she shied! She put her head down and she snorted! She took the bit in her teeth and tore off over the fields. And Towhead went wild, too! He galloped off with his mother, raring and tearing and plunging! There was a runaway for you! The Old Man couldn't control 'em. He hollered, "Whoa, there! Whoa!" but they dragged him along by the reins till he stubbed his toe on a stump, fell down flat on his stomach, and lost the reins out of his hand.

Not till they were all worn out, did Towhead and the Old Woman quiet down again.

THROUGH THE GATE

Well, when all this was over, the Old Man picked up the paper that had scared his team so badly. It was a piece of newspaper and that was a great surprise! Before this he'd been thinking that he had the state of Texas almost to himself; but, if he had found a newspaper, there must be people near. Sure enough! He found he had neighbors not two-days' journey away.

"We're moving west," he said to his family, "where a man can breathe free and easy without having other folks cramp him and squeeze him and hem him in!"

So he loaded up his wagon with all their household goods, but he thought he wouldn't try hitching Towhead and the Old Woman to such a load as this. Wild horses would be better. Out he went on the plains and caught a couple of raring, tearing, snorting Texas mustangs. He hitched 'em up to the wagon; then he stuffed the Old Woman and ten of the younger children, counting Baby Bill, into the wagon, too.

The Old Man and the oldest boys walked by the horses' heads and they set out to go further westward. They went along without mishap till they came to the Pecos River. There the horses plunged into the water, splashing and spattering and dripping. They were going up the other bank when the end of the wagon gave way. That wagon was just so plumb full of household goods and of children bursting out this way and that, that it couldn't stand the strain forever. The end-board got pushed out and Baby Bill, who was sitting on the very edge of the wagon, fell down kerplunk to the ground. The Old Man and the

Old Woman never noticed that he was gone. They had so many children that they never stopped to count noses more than once in four weeks, and they didn't miss Baby Bill till the next nose-counting came, three weeks from the following Tuesday, and then they had gone so far they couldn't turn back again.

THROUGH THE GATE

Well, Baby Bill looked around and found himself all alone in a big world of sage brush and cactus. He was lost in the Pecos country and, ever after that, he was called Pecos Bill. Toddling along up the bank he was getting mighty hungry when he met a nice-looking, motherly, hard-working mother Coyote, one of those big prairie wolves that roam around in the West. Mrs. Coyote looked Bill over and she took a liking to him; so she told him to jump on her back and she carried him home to her burrow, the hole in the ground where she lived with her lively coyote pups. Pretty soon Bill was playing with those wild little coyote pups as if they were brothers and sisters. They were a mischievous lot and plenty of pranks they played on the long-suffering Mrs. Coyote. Bill learned to talk their language, and he lived exactly as they did.

Soon he was running with the pack, hunting deer
and jack rabbits and chasing over the plains, yipping
and yapping and yelling; and he'd sit on a hill in the
nighttime, howling to the big round moon for all the
world like a coyote. In fact he was so very little when
he went to live with the coyotes, that he thought he
was a coyote and no doubt at all about it. He lived as
one of the pack until he was ten years old.

But one day when he was ten, an old cowboy came
loping along, riding at an easy pace through the Pecos
River country on a nice little black pony. He saw Bill
running around through the sage brush and cactus, not
wearing a stitch of clothing, as naked as when he was
born. So he called to the boy and
said: "Who be you, little feller?"

Bill peeked out from the sage brush
and he answered: "I'm a coyote!"

But the cowboy said: "Coyote,
nothin'! You jest can't be a coyote."

"Don't I go naked?" asked
Bill, coming up a little closer.
"That's what the coyotes do,
so you see I must be a coyote."

"Injuns go naked," said the
cowboy. "And Injuns are men,
they're not coyotes!"

"Well, then, I howl!" cried Bill.
"You see, I must be a coyote!"

198

"But men howl, too," said the cowboy. "Most pertickaler men in Texas!"

"Anyhow, I'm a coyote!" Bill started to run away. "Now, little feller, see here," the cowboy called him back. "If you were really a coyote, you would have a tail. All the coyotes have tails. Have you got a tail? I ask you!"

"I never thought of that," said Bill and he looked around over his shoulder. Sure enough, it was true, he didn't have any tail.

"Then I'm not a coyote," he said. "What in the world can I be?"

"You're a man-child, that's what!" said the cowboy. "And you'd better stop runnin' with coyotes. You better come along with me and go back where men are men!"

So that's how Pecos Bill went back to the cowtowns and cowcamps of the cattle-raising country.

He learned to ride any horse. Not the wildest wild broncho could throw him. He learned how to round up cattle and how to sling his rope to lasso whole herds at a time. One day he was sitting alone high up on a mountain-top when he looked down and saw a railroad train running along below. It was huffing and puffing and snorting, so Bill, having never in all his life seen a railroad train before, thought it was some strange critter. He slung his rope and he roped it! He dragged it clean up in the air almost to the mountain-top. But while it was dangling there some friends of Bill's came along and told him what it was and that there were people in it. So Bill dropped the train down gently and set it back on its track.

Bill could fight rattlesnakes, too. Once, when he took off his boots and lay down to sleep for a little under a forty-foot cactus, two enormous rattlers crawled into his boots and hid. When he woke up again and went to put on his boots, those snakes began to rattle. They stuck out their fangs to strike. But Bill grabbed one in each hand and he shook the day-lights out of them. Then he tied their tails together and slung 'em over a tree where he let 'em stay for

awhile, thinkin' over their sins till they said they were sorry for their crimes and ready to be good snakes. Then he took them down and untied them. He put one around his neck in place of the bright red handkerchief most of the cowboys wear and he used the other for a quirt to whip up his bucking broncho.

There wasn't an ugly steer, a bad-acting horse, or an Indian who could get away with anything if Bill was on the job. He hunted great herds of buffalo, he wrestled with grizzly bears, and he fought all the horse thieves and robbers. He went after badmen so hard that he had them just scared to death.

Bill was none of your two-gun men! Bill was a four-gun man! He could shoot four pistols at once, one with each of his hands, and one with each of his feet where he kept them hitched to his stirrups. All the robbers were afraid of him and soon took leave of the state. Texas was so cleaned up, there wasn't much left to do. So Bill began to think he'd better head further westward and clean up that country, too. He made up his mind to be boss of the toughest outfit of hard-riding, straight-shooting, roaring cowboys that ever came skally-hooting into a dusty cowtown and to wage a war to the finish with the badmen of the land. So he saddled up his horse and started out for New Mexico.

Riding along on his way he sang a cowboy song:

"Oh, for me a horse and saddle,
Every day without a change;
With the desert sun a blazin'
On a hundred miles of range.
Just a-ridin', just a-ridin',
Desert ripplin' in the sun,
Mountains blue along the skyline,—
I don't envy anyone."

THROUGH THE GATE

Bill was singing like that when he met a trapper who said just the kind of tough outfit Bill wanted, was camping on up the trail beyond a rocky canyon. Bill was hurrying on toward the camp when his horse stubbed his toe and fell.  He fell down and broke his neck. That was a blow, I'm telling you. Bill loved that horse like a pal. Often enough at night when those two were all alone, riding the range or the trail, Bill had talked to his horse as if he'd been a human. But there wasn't a thing to do so far as the horse was concerned. He'd gone to the horses' heaven.

So Bill made the best of matters. He took off the horse's saddle, slung it over his shoulder and walked along up the trail. Pretty soon he heard a noise and looking up all at once he saw two big, round eyes staring from the underbrush growing on a rock above. Quick as lightning, something sprang out, whizzing along through the air. It pounced right down on top of him. A big mountain lion it was, the terror of all the district. Bill set to wrestling at once and he gave that mountain lion the licking of his young life. He threw him this way and that till the lion was tame as a cat. Then he put his saddle on the critter and rode him, whooping and yelling, down through the rocky canyon, swinging his rattlesnake quirt, and making the big cat leap a hundred feet at a jump.

Soon he saw a chuckwagon with a bunch of cowboys nearby around their campfire eating. Splitting the air with his war whoops, his lion screeching and spitting, his rattlesnakes singing their rattles, he rode up to the fire, grabbed his lion by the ear, drew him back on his haunches, stepped off him, and looked at the outfit. The cowboys just sat, their mouths open, saying nothing at all. Spying a big pot of beans cooking over the fire, Bill reached in his hands, took out two sizzling handfuls and swallowed them down red hot. Then he seized a kettle of coffee and drank it down still boiling. After that he said:

"Who is the boss around here?"

A big fellow eight feet tall with seven guns and nine bowie knives bristling around in his belt, stood up and took off his hat.

"Who is the boss around here?" He seemed kind of stunned as he spoke. "Stranger, I *was*, but you *be*!" The big man bowed his head and all the other cowboys acknowledged Bill as their boss.

So that's how Bill got the outfit that worked under him in New Mexico, rounding up millions of cattle, riding the big western ranges and dealing out death to badmen.

His good friends were Alkali Ike; Cheyenne Charley; the Arizona Kid; Bullfrog Doyle, the dancer; and Pretty Pete Rogers, the best-dressed man at rodeos and dances. You should have seen Pretty Pete! With his silver-ornamented bridle, his silver-ornamented saddle, his grizzly-bear chaps, big Stetson hat, high-heeled boots and silver spurs, Pretty Pete was something to look at! He'd swing the girls at dances and have them as thick as flies crowding round him at barbecues. Leaping Lena and Pitching Sal, handsome Covered-Wagon Lizz and lovely Rocking-chair Emma had eyes for no other cowboy when Pretty Pete went to a hoedown.

But the best pal Bill had in the world was a man named Curley Joe, a curley-headed fellow with legs bowed out like a wishbone from riding so much on horseback. How Bill did love Curley Joe! The two had sworn to be friends till that fierce old Indian chief, Sitting Bull, should stand up! And that, in the cowboy's language, meant forever and ever.

But one day a terrible thing happened to Curley Joe. Bill's pet horse was a broncho no one but Bill could ride.

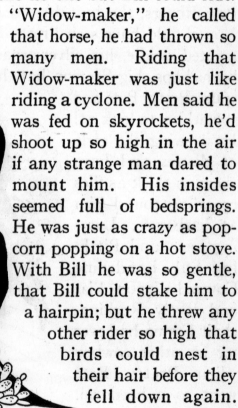

"Widow-maker," he called that horse, he had thrown so many men. Riding that Widow-maker was just like riding a cyclone. Men said he was fed on skyrockets, he'd shoot up so high in the air if any strange man dared to mount him. His insides seemed full of bedsprings. He was just as crazy as pop-corn popping on a hot stove. With Bill he was so gentle, that Bill could stake him to a hairpin; but he threw any other rider so high that birds could nest in their hair before they fell down again.

THROUGH THE GATE

Well, Curley Joe had a hankering to ride that Widow-maker. He said he had never in all his life seen horse-flesh he couldn't ride and he'd bet he could stick on that broncho like a horsefly on a mule's ear. Bill begged him not to try it, but Joe kept teasing and teasing till at last Bill shook his head and said, "All right, you can try!"

So the cowboys all stood around while Joe tried to mount the horse, with Widow-maker looking sidewise out of a wicked eye. And they sang at the top of their lungs:

"Ride him, you cowboy, ride him!—
Say, you are sure on some hoss!
Keep on a-settin' astride him
Till he has learnt who is boss!"

But the very moment when Joe got up at last on his back, Widow-maker put down his head and biff! he kicked the lid off! He threw Curley Joe so high that he shot up just like fireworks! He sailed along through the air, up and up and up till he lit on the top of Pike's Peak. Bill saw it all through a spyglass. He saw Curley Joe come down on the very tip-top of Pike's Peak. He saw him sitting there on a rock as pointed as a needle with cliffs falling down below him, steep and smooth as glass. He hadn't a chance to get down. And there was snow on the cliffs, big patches of shiny white snow, making the air as cold as a blizzard at the North Pole. Curley Joe sat there freezing, shivering, and shaking and starving.

THROUGH THE GATE

Well, Bill felt very sad. He watched Curley Joe through his spyglass wondering what he could do till he happened to think of his rope. He ran for that rope in a jiffy. He shook out the noose with a jerk, he whirled it about his head in big enormous circles—faster and faster and faster. Then, zip, he let it go with his eyes fastened straight on Pike's Peak. Sure enough, that rope slipped 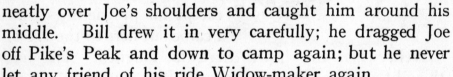 neatly over Joe's shoulders and caught him around his middle. Bill drew it in very carefully; he dragged Joe off Pike's Peak and down to camp again; but he never let any friend of his ride Widow-maker again.

Bill rode the plains for years, rounding up his cattle, sleeping under the stars, dashing into the cowtowns, and ridding the land of badmen. But one day on the range, he was driving his little dogies—as cowboys call their cattle—and singing at the top of his voice:

"Whoopee ti-yi-yo, git along little dogies."

All of a sudden he saw a little dude from the East with a great big pair of spectacles, limping along up the road because he was sore from riding. He was leading a rat-tailed old plug with his ribs sticking out like bedslats. Bill could see at a glance that that dude couldn't ride a thing wilder than a wheel chair or a baby carriage; but his face was

half-hidden from sight under a big Stetson hat, and he was wearing chaps and a suit of cowboy's clothes bought from a mail-order store. When he heard Bill singing, "Git along little dogies," he stopped politely and said: "I heard that song back East, but I wish you'd tell me, sir, where you keep your doggies. I haven't seen a single dog except for prairie dogs, since I came out here to the West!"

Well, when Bill heard that, he laughed. The man thought dogies were doggies! Bill laughed and he laughed and he laughed. And he looked at that poor little dude lost in his cowboy clothes and he laughed and he laughed again. He laughed and he laughed and he laughed, till he laughed himself to death. And that was a proper end for a man like Pecos Bill.

In the rocks of Arizona, you can still see in places the footprints of Bill's big horses; and the great white spots in the desert that men call alkali lakes, are really the baking powder left in the big mixing-bowls his cooks dug out in the ground when they made baking-powder biscuits to feed all that huge outfit of straight-shooting, hard-riding cowboys that followed Pecos Bill.

THE COWBOY'S LIFE*

THE bawl of a steer,
  To a cowboy's ear,
Is music of sweetest strain;
And the yelping notes
Of the gray coyotes
To him are a glad refrain.

The rapid beat
Of his broncho's feet
On the sod as he speeds along,
Keeps living time
To the ringing rhyme
Of his rollicking cowboy song.

—*American Cowboy Song*

*Songs made by cowboys riding the prairies or sung around fires in cow-camps, are real American folk music, full of the rhythm of hoofbeats, the sound of the coyotes' call, and wind in the sage brush.

THE PLANTING OF THE APPLE TREE
WILLIAM CULLEN BRYANT

WHAT plant we in this apple tree?
  Buds, which the breath of summer days
Shall lengthen into leafy sprays;
Boughs where the thrush, with crimson breast,
Shall haunt and sing and hide her nest;
We plant, upon the sunny lea,
A shadow for the noontide hour,
A shelter from the summer shower,
  When we plant the apple tree.

What plant we in this apple tree?
Fruits that shall swell in sunny June,
And redden in the August noon,
And drop, when gentle airs come by,
That fan the blue September sky,
  While children come, with cries of glee,
And seek them where the fragrant grass
Betrays their bed to those who pass,
  At the foot of the apple tree.

Old Johnny Appleseed*

A LEGEND OF THE MIDDLE WEST

A HUNDRED years ago, when the early settlers of Ohio lived in little log cabins out in the lonely wilderness, a very queer, old man used to wander from farm to farm. Johnny Appleseed, he was called, though his real name was John Chapman. Along the old wagon trail between the rows of young corn, Johnny would come tramping up to the door of some farmhouse, merrily whistling a tune and dressed in nothing whatever except an old coffee sack with holes for his arms and legs. As a hat, he wore a tin pan in which he cooked his mush, with a homemade pasteboard contraption sticking out in front to protect his eyes from the sun. Usually, he was barefooted. Only when snow lay deep on the great forests or the prairies, was he sometimes to be seen with a castoff boot on one foot and a moccasin on the other. Aye, he was queer, all right! Yet no one ever laughed at Johnny. The people loved him too dearly. He would bring the little girls ribbons and small gay pieces of calico, wonderful playthings in those days when everyone had so little. The children tagged at his heels wherever he appeared.

*The story of Johnny Appleseed, who came west about 1800, to plant apple seeds that future generations might enjoy the fruit, has become an American legend of pioneer days with all the persistence of a folk tale.

Often he mended old tinware as he talked to the farmers' wives and everyone was glad to see him, for life was very lonely and visitors brought news.

Years ago, Johnny had given a poor woman, with a large family, his home at Pittsburgh Landing. He had a great idea! There was something he wanted to do! Lashing two canoes together, he packed them with deer-skin bags filled full of apple seeds. Then he drifted off with the current down the Ohio River. He had a secret plan; he would make people more at home in the lonely western wilderness by planting apple trees!

Farms were far apart in those days, separated by miles of billowy, treeless prairies or shadowy old forests, where bears, deer, wolves, and Indians often wandered about. Men, women, and children toiled hard to raise the sim-plest food; and, for fruit, they had only berries and sour wild plums or crabs. They had no friendly apple trees to comfort them of an evening with juicy, round, red apples, munched by all the family about the open fire. Often the hearts of those pioneers were heavy with homesick longing, as they thought of the low, rambling farmhouses left far away in the East, so cozy and so peaceful beneath the pink-and-white glory of blossoming apple trees.

Old Johnny knew how they felt. Old Johnny knew what they wanted. He liked nothing better in life than to wander off in the wilderness and plant his precious seeds. Every year, he gathered the seeds that were thrown away from the ciderpresses in Western Pennsylvania. Then he tramped back with his load all the way to Ohio.

Often people said to Johnny: "Aren't you afraid to wander about barefooted?" Other men wrapped their legs in bandages of dried grass to protect them from the sting of the many poisonous snakes that abounded in the tall grass. But Johnny only replied: "I love every one of God's creatures!" And so he tramped through the forest, fearless, safe, and free. Mother bears let him play with their cubs, and even the Indians loved him.

In the war of 1812, when the red men broke out savagely against the lone white settlers along the frontiers of the West, they still let Johnny go freely through the narrow trails of the woods. And, though he did not fight, he often wandered for days, giving word to the settlers that the Indians were on the warpath and warning them to flee to the nearest blockhouse for safety. Suddenly, he would appear out of the depth of the forest thundering forth his message like a prophet out of the Bible:

"The spirit of the Lord is upon me and He hath anointed me to sound an alarm in the forest; for behold, the tribes of the heathen are round about your doors!"

With all his heart Johnny believed that God had sent him forth to preach the gospel of love and to plant his apple seeds. When he came to a cabin at nightfall and the family sat about the fire, he would stretch himself out on the floor and ask the little group if they wished to hear "some news right fresh from Heaven." Then he would take out his Bible and read the words of Jesus.

Slowly many people came pressing into the wilderness. Towns and churches appeared and stagecoaches broke—with the blare of their horns—the ancient, peaceful stillness of prairies and age-old forests.

So in 1858, Johnny said farewell to his friends and turned his face farther westward to spend his last nine years still in advance of settlement, far on the frontier. And when, after forty years, his long, unselfish labors came at last to an end, how richly they had borne fruit! One-hundred-thousand square miles in Ohio, Indiana, and parts of Illinois bore witness to the labors of one stout-hearted old hero, who planted his little brown seeds in order that men and women, youths and maids and children, whom he would never see, should some day eat rosy apples around their glowing hearths and wander in the Springtime beneath the fragrantly blossoming apple trees.

The Pert Fire Engine*

GELETT BURGESS

THERE were many fire engines, members of the Fire Department of the City o' Ligg, but of all the number, the most ill-behaved was the disreputable little Number Four. He was known all over the city as the black sheep of the flock, and everyone knew the stories of his mischief.

In spite of his evil deeds he was a very handsome machine, wearing a pretty coat of enamel and all his fittings were nickeled, so that they shone like silver buttons. He always had silken hose, too, for he was very rich. But he usually was the last engine at the fire, and he was always sure to shirk. He would hold back when he was signalled to "*Play away, Four*," and he would squirt a stream strong enough to drench the Chief, when he should have held back. He consumed an enormous amount of the most expensive fuel, and he wheezed and puffed till the air shook with vibrations. He could have been the best engine in the fire department if he had wanted to, but he didn't.

*From *The Lively City o' Ligg.* Reprinted by special arrangement with the publishers, Frederick A. Stokes Company.

THROUGH THE GATE

So the people of the City o' Ligg were not very much surprised when they heard that Number Four had run away. They hoped only that he would stay away, for they could get along much better without him. "He's more trouble than he's worth," said an old ladder-

cart. "I've been tempted more than once to fall on him and break his boiler for him. He wouldn't even have his hose darned, because he prefers to leak all over the street!"

For a few weeks Number Four enjoyed his truancy. He spent most of his time down by a lake, a little outside the city, and there he amused himself by going in swimming and squirting water over himself like an elephant, till he shone brilliantly in the sun- shine. When he was tired of that, he went around to the farmhouses and sucked all the water out of their wells and flooded their cellars. The stables were all very much afraid of him; but dared not complain, though they told their fences to catch him if they could.

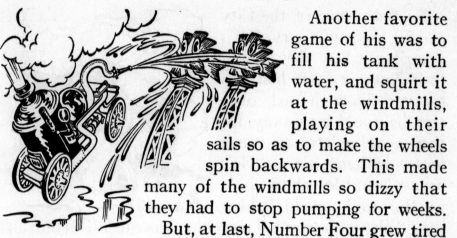

Another favorite game of his was to fill his tank with water, and squirt it at the windmills, playing on their sails so as to make the wheels spin backwards. This made many of the windmills so dizzy that they had to stop pumping for weeks.

But, at last, Number Four grew tired of this mischief in the country and he began to cast about for something more exciting to do. So, one night, he loaded himself with water and rolled into the City o' Ligg.

He drew up before a two-story house that was not painted, but only whitewashed, and began to squirt water all over her. The poor little house shut all her doors and windows, but even then she was drenched to the skin; and after an hour or so, almost all the whitewash was soaked off, and she stood cold, dripping and shivering in the night air with her naked boards streaked with white. The naughty fire engine laughed brutally at her distress and went back to the lake to concoct more mischief.

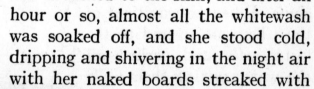

THROUGH THE GATE

Every night after that, Number Four went into the town and drenched the houses, laughing as he poured streams of cold water down their chimneys, breaking their windows, washing away their foundations, and splashing them all over with muddy water.

At last it got to be altogether too much to endure, and the houses consulted together to see how Number Four could be caught and punished. They could think of no way, however, and so, after the fire engine had showered a very old and respectable church and given it a severe cold, they applied to the telegraph office to help them.

The telegraph office was by far the cleverest building in the City o' Ligg, but it took him some time to think of a remedy for this trouble. He consulted, by wire, with all the offices around Ligg, and at last they decided upon a plan.

Notice was sent to all the telegraph poles to strip off their wires and come into Ligg for further orders. The next day the houses were surprised to see a procession of long, naked telegraph poles march into town, each with a roll of wire on his arm. They marched up to the telegraph office that night and received their instructions.

As soon as it was dark, the poles separated this way and that, some going to one part of the town, and some to another, till the whole city was surrounded. For several hours, while the houses slept in peace, the poles worked, going in and out with the wires till they had woven a fence all round the town. At the principal entrances, they left the streets free for the fire engine to get in; but they contrived big V-shaped traps here and there, which could be closed by the poles at a moment's notice. By this time it was twelve o'clock, the hour when Number Four usually appeared; and, when all the town was quiet, the poles waited for the bad engine to come.

At last they heard the rumble of wheels on the road from the lake and, in the dark, they saw a bright light approaching. It was the fire in the naughty engine, who was puffing his way into the town, chuckling to himself over the fun he was to have with the Town Hall that night, for he had planned to fill the whole of the third story with water before he came back. Number Four came up to the city gate, with no suspicion of what was awaiting him, and boldly rolled up the main avenue past the double line of sleeping houses. There was one house that was snoring with a rough noise, and the fire engine turned with a laugh and sent a stream of water through the window.

Suddenly the telegraph poles closed round him; they waved and towered over his head; they lay on the ground across his road; they threatened to fall upon him. The poor engine was terrified out of his senses. He backed and jumped, he whistled and groaned, and he spouted a black column of smoke out of his funnel and sent streams of water in every direction. Suddenly, seeing an opening, he darted back toward the gate, but he soon found himself walled in by the wire fences. He tried another way and another, but there was no escape; the wires hemmed him in on all sides, till he finally was stuck so fast that he could not move and he

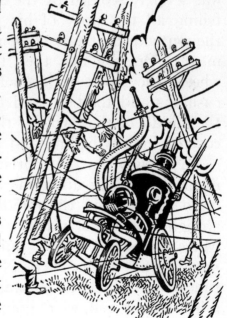

stood panting, waiting to see what would happen next.

His wheels were tied and his fires put out; and, the next morning, the poor, shame-faced engine was pulled into town past the lines of houses who jeered at him scornfully. He was led into the Park in the center of the City o' Ligg, and there, where all the principal buildings could see, he was severely scolded by the Mayor. It was a long lecture, telling all the story of his wickedness, and ending with the sentence that was to be inflicted upon him as punishment. One by one they took off his bright, red-gold wheels; they took off his pole and whipple-trees, his seat-cushions and toolbox; and then they dug a deep hole in the middle of the Park by the side of a well, put him in, covered him with dirt, and sodded over the burial place.

And now when the tourists in the City o' Ligg compliment the Mayor upon the beautiful fountain that plays night and day in the middle of the Park, sending up a straight stream of water a hundred feet in the air, the Mayor says: "Oh, yes; quite so, quite so! That is the naughty fire engine, little Number Four, working out his time of punishment. He was put in for twenty years; but, if he behaves well, we're going to let him out in nineteen!"